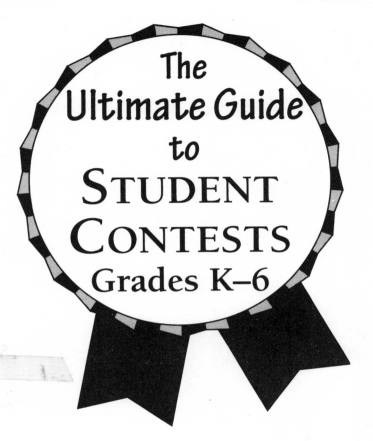

The Ultimate Guide to STUDENT CONTESTS
Grades K–6

Also by Scott Pendleton
The Ultimate Guide to Student Contests, Grades 7–12

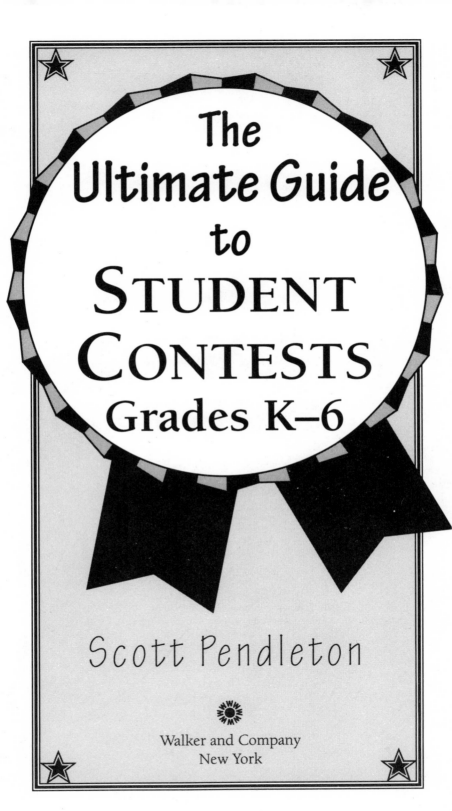

The Ultimate Guide to STUDENT CONTESTS
Grades K–6

Scott Pendleton

Walker and Company
New York

First published in the United States of America in 1998 by Walker
Publishing Company, Inc.

Published simultaneously in Canada by Thomas Allen & Son Canada,
Limited, Markham, Ontario

Library of Congress Cataloging-in-Publication Data
Pendleton, Scott, 1955–
The ultimate guide to student contests, grades K–6/Scott
Pendleton.
p.   cm.
Includes index.
ISBN 0-8027-7513-6 (pbk.)
1. School contests—United States—Directories.   2. Education,
Elementary—United States.   I. Title.
LB3068.P452   1997
370'.79—dc21   97-25545
CIP

BOOK DESIGN BY CAROL MALCOLM RUSSO/SIGNET M DESIGN, INC.

PRINTED IN THE UNITED STATES OF AMERICA
2   4   6   8   10   9   7   5   3   1

Contents

Acknowledgments

Many organizations and individuals work very hard to give students the opportunity to enjoy academic competitions. Thanks for your effort and for your help with this book. I hope the book facilitates your work and attracts more students to your worthwhile events.

Thanks to Alan Kellock, a patient, encouraging, and unfailingly professional agent. Thanks also to Liza Miller and Jackie Johnson at Walker and Company for diligently reading the manuscript and for coordinating the art and other details.

Many family members provided encouragement. Thanks to Monte and Linda Pendleton; to Charlotte and Lynn McNamee; to Emma and Marina; and most of all to Virginia, the very best wife for me.

Introduction

Is it fun when your teacher says, "Test on Friday"? No way. But what if your teacher were to say, "Whoever does the best in this contest wins a trip to Space Camp"? Now we're talking fun!

Contests are exciting and challenging. They introduce you to new ideas and new friends. They might allow you to travel and even to win a prize! But winning isn't the point; trying is. In every contest, you will surprise yourself by doing more than you thought you could. That's a nice feeling. It makes you want to jump right back in and try some more.

As you look through these contest listings, you'll find some that only elementary school students may enter. Others are also open to older kids and even adults; yet sometimes the elementary school kids win those events as well, many contest organizers say. So go ahead—enter! One film festival organizer, eager to receive student entries, quoted this remark from famous movie director Francis Ford Coppola: "Some little girl in Ohio is going to pick up a camera and become the next Mozart of film!" It could be you!

Frequently Asked Questions

Am I eligible?

That's easy to figure out. Pick any contest listing and look at the very next line after the contest name. There you'll see any eligibility restrictions, such as the exclusion of noncitizens, home-schooled students, or one gender or the other.

If that line contains address information, then no special restrictions apply. That means the contest is open (but not necessarily limited) to: (1) kids who are either *U.S. citizens* living anywhere in the world or noncitizens who are *permanent U.S. residents,* and (2) kids either in *grades K to 6* or *between the ages of six and twelve.*

Since this book is for students twelve years old and younger, I have made twelve (or sixth grade) the cutoff age even when a contest is also open to older kids. For example, a contest for fifth to eighth grades is listed as "grades 5–6" and one for ages nine to fourteen is listed as "ages 9–12." (Older kids can read *The Ultimate Guide to Student Contests, Grades 7–12.*) Kids younger than six are eligible to enter contests described as "up to age 12" and "all ages" (see next question).

Do I really have a chance to win?

Even in contests open to older kids, the organizers clearly expect elementary school students to stand a chance of doing well. Otherwise they would exclude you at the outset. Most even have a division for your grade or age group.

However, contests marked "all ages" are not specifically intended for students. You will compete against adults. Do you stand a chance against experienced, trained grown-ups? Maybe. Organizers of contests from poetry to robot building all have stories of the time an elementary school student trounced highly qualified adults. (In one case the embarrassed adults threatened legal action but still couldn't overturn the results.)

Even when they don't win, ambitious youngsters impress judges by daring to compete with adults. And they gain experience. That has far more value than a trophy on the mantelpiece.

Remember, if you wanted to win the Indy 500, you wouldn't wait to enter until you were the oldest race car driver around. Neither should you worry about your age when entering these academic contests.

One more thing. You don't have to be the world's best to win, just the best among those who enter. A comedian once said that 80 percent of success in life is just showing up. Funny, and also surprisingly true. For instance, hundreds of thousands of students will never hear about these contests. Thousands more will hear, but will decide not to enter for whatever reason. Only a relative few "go for the gold."

This much is certain: If you do not enter, you will not win. But if you do enter, you will have a rewarding experience, whether the reward is a new computer or just a great time and fun new friends. And you'll be better prepared for next year's event.

What do the contest listings tell me?

The basics: what the contest is about, how to get more information, restrictions on eligibility, deadlines, entry fees, and prizes. Some listings are cross-references to related listings in the same or another chapter.

Samples of winning work are given with some art and writing contest listings. If you look at the samples and think, "Hey, I could do *that*," then you've gotten the point of this book. Now prove it.

Do I have to contact the contest organizers?

Always! Deadlines, size requirements, themes, and so on can change from year to year. And some of the simplest-sounding contests have reams of fine print. The organizer can best give you the full scoop.

Sometimes this book does get fairly specific about things like word counts for stories or dimensions for artwork. That's so you can see whether something that you have already created could be submitted to a contest. But the listings may omit other details that could disqualify your entry, like whether your name goes in the upper-right corner or upper-left corner of your poem—no joke. So be sure always to call or write for submission guidelines.

You should also visit http://www.studentcontests.com/, the Web site for this book. That's the place to get new addresses for contest organizers, learn about new contests, and see prizewinning entries that we couldn't reproduce here, like videos and musical compositions.

When should I contact the organizers?

Why wait? Do it now—unless the listing says to limit inquiries to a certain time of year. In cases like that, write the letter and mark on the envelope when to mail it. Then post it on your refrigerator so you won't forget to mail it when the time comes. The organizer will respond even to letters that arrive smelling like peanut butter.

Should I send an SASE (self-addressed, stamped envelope)?

Yes, when writing to magazines or organizers of creative writing contests. Those folks pinch their pennies.

Some contests are supported by foundations or businesses. Don't send them an SASE unless they ask for one. They usually do not mind paying for postage. Often they mail you materials that wouldn't fit into a business envelope anyway.

When in doubt, send an SASE. It can't hurt, it guarantees you'll hear back, and it doesn't cost much. But don't overlook other possibilities for getting the information, like visiting contests' Web sites, sending them E-mail, or calling their toll-free telephone numbers.

Are there some contests that require teacher or class participation?

Yes, although most of the contests in this book allow you to enter on your own without teacher assistance. Look for this icon 🐾 at the beginning of all contests that require you to enter with your class or through the sponsorship of your teacher.

I'm a parent. What should I do?

Rejoice! You found this book. *The Ultimate Guide to Student Contests* puts a wealth of educational activities for your kindergartner through sixth grader at your fingertips. Participation in student contests enables high achievers to test themselves as never before. And for kids who haven't yet found a reason to relish school, contests can spark an enthusiasm for learning that they'll carry back to the classroom.

Many appealing events await the kids who explore this book. Make sure yours turn these pages. Scan the book yourself. Call attention to contests likely to captivate your kids.

Suppose, though, that it was your son or daughter who brought this book home. No matter how eager, kids take signals from adults. Make sure your kids know that you are committed to helping them participate fully in the contests they choose. It's also a good idea to explore contest Web sites with your child, especially any that are "for all ages." A site that posts work from teenagers and adults may have content unsuitable for a young child.

When it comes to money, most contests require little or none. A few events are restricted to schools that pay an annual fee, or to students of teachers who pay dues to a professional organization. If the school or teacher can't cover the cost, then find a community sponsor, hold a fund-raiser, or try splitting the fee with other parents.

As for time, some contests require a little involvement by a local adult to supervise or serve as a point of contact. Volunteer! This is your chance to make a positive impact in our educational system. It's also a chance to interact with kids in a constructive activity of their choice (unlike, say, making their beds or taking out the trash).

Assured of adult assistance, kids will more likely send off for entry forms. To be on the safe side, sit down with your child and help with writing to the contest organizers. Walk him or her, letter in hand, to the corner mailbox. Drop the envelope inside. There! Maybe for the first time, he or she has initiated an education-enhancing activity. That's reason enough to celebrate. And there will be more as your child continues the grand adventure in learning that comes from participation in academic contests.

The
Ultimate Guide
to
STUDENT
CONTESTS
Grades K–6

1

Grand Openings
Art, Dance and Music,
Film/Video, and Photography

What's that in your hand? A paintbrush? A clarinet? A shutter-release? Here are the events for you artists, dancers, musicians, filmmakers, and photographers to express yourselves and impress the rest of us!

Art

American Morgan Horse Association Contests

Up to age 12
Write: American Morgan Horse Association
P.O. Box 960
Shelburne, VT 05482-0960
E-mail: info@morganhorse.com
Internet: http://www.morganhorse.com/
Call: Erica Richard, Director, Youth Programs

Main: 802-985-4944
Direct: 802-985-1260, ext. 25
Fax: 802-985-8897

Love horses? Display your affection for the Morgan breed through writing, photography, or art of any kind.

1. AMHA MORGAN HORSE ART CONTEST
Pay $2 per artwork to enter. All art becomes the property of AMHA. You will not get it back. AMHA may use the art for promotional purposes and auction it at the annual convention. Entries must be postmarked no later than the first of October. The first-place winner in the junior division (ages seventeen and under) receives a $40 gift certificate.

2. AMHAY PHOTO CONTEST
Submit five-by-seven-inch or eight-by-ten-inch prints, either black-and-white or color. Pay $2 per photo to enter. AMHA may reproduce

Morgan Farm by Priscilla Pietz, 12, Valley Park, Missouri, fifth-place winner in the 1996 American Morgan Horse Association Contests. Courtesy of American Morgan Horse Association.

the photos for promotional purposes and auction them at the annual convention. Entries must be postmarked no later than the first of October. Prizes are $50 and $25.

AMVETS Contests

Write: AMVETS
Program National Headquarters
4647 Forbes Boulevard
Lanham, MD 20706-4380
Call: Dave Tyler
Main: 301-459-9600
Fax: 301-459-7924

AMVETS has 180,000 members, including men and women who served honorably or still serve in the U.S. military. The organization assists veterans and promotes the American way of life.

Local contests are held in the spring. Contact your AMVETS chapter for specific deadlines and contest themes. Local winners advance to state-level competition and then the national competition in July.

1. NATIONAL AMERICANISM AMERICAN FLAG POSTER DRAWING CONTEST

Grade 4

The theme is always the American flag: fifty stars on a field of blue, seven red stripes, and six white ones. Use paint, crayons, watercolors, or colored pencils on construction paper or posterboard. Your entry must be done freehand; no artificial stars, stencils, or tracing allowed. Size limit is eleven and a half inches by fifteen inches.

National prizes are U.S. Savings Bonds worth $150, $100, and $50.

2. NATIONAL AMERICANISM POSTER DRAWING CONTEST

Grades 3 and 5

Create art based on the year's theme. In 1996 it was "What Does an American Veteran Mean to me?" Use pen, pencil, crayon, paint, or a combination of those media on construction paper or posterboard. Your entry must be done freehand; no gluing pictures or other materials to your poster. Size limit is eleven and a half inches by fifteen inches. Write up to fifty words describing your art directly on the back of your poster.

National prizes are U.S. Savings Bonds worth $150, $100, and $50.

❦ Arbor Day National Poster Contest

Grade 5
Write: National Arbor Day Foundation
P.O. Box 85784
Lincoln, NE 68508
Internet: http://www.arborday.org/teaching/poster_contest.html
Call: Michelle Saulnier-Scribner, National Coordinator
Main: 402-474-5655

Americans have celebrated Arbor Day for 125 years in recognition of the importance of trees. Each year a million fifth graders in 34,000 classrooms express themselves on a tree-related theme selected by the National Arbor Day Foundation for their annual poster contest. The 1997 theme was "Trees Are Terrific . . . Arbor Day Is Too! 125 Years of Stewardship."

To participate, students must live in a state that has a contest coordinator (forty-two states did in 1996). Check with your state's natural history or forestry department or the National Arbor Day Foundation's Web site for current contact information.

Each September the coordinators send Arbor Day curriculum kits, which detail activities leading up to the national poster contest, to a

Artwork by Brittany Pruitt, 5th grade, Honea Path, South Carolina, the 1997 grand-prize winner of the Arbor Day National Poster Contest. Courtesy of National Arbor Day Foundation.

designated number of classrooms in their state. (Home schools can request to participate.) The coordinators also organize the state contests.

Winning state posters are submitted to the foundation by the first Tuesday in April. One national winner is chosen. The prize is a $500 savings bond for the student and $200 cash for the student's teacher. The student, a parent, and the teacher receive an expenses-paid trip to Nebraska City, Nebraska, to participate in National Arbor Day festivities (the last Friday in April). The student winner rides in a parade and attends an award banquet.

Children's Turtle Conservation Poster Contest

Grades K–6
Write: New York Turtle and Tortoise Society

Artwork by Megan McCoy, 2nd grade, Sayville, New York, the 1993 grand-prize winner of the Children's Turtle Conservation Poster Contest. Photo by Allen Salzberg. Courtesy of New York Turtle and Tortoise Society.

Attn: Lorri Cramer
750 Columbus Avenue
New York, NY 10025
E-mail: ASalzberg@aol.com
Call: Lorri Cramer, Contest Coordinator
Direct: 212-459-4803
Fax: 718-275-3307

The world has over 260 turtle species, 100 of which need serious conservation attention. Help spread awareness by creating a poster that depicts their plight.

You may focus on a particular species or on turtles in general. Subject matter may be anything from threats to turtles' survival to ideas for helping them repopulate, such as proposals for cleaning streams or controlling habitat destruction. Use heavyweight posterboard measuring either twelve by eighteen inches or eighteen by twenty-four inches. Posters with other dimensions will be disqualified. You can use paint, magic markers, colored inks, or collage. Check with the contest coordinator before using other materials.

On the back of your poster, clearly print your name, address, phone number, age, grade, and the name of your school (if applicable). Entries are grouped according to age or grade level.

Posters must be mailed between January 1 and April 15. A panel of conservationists, artists, and teachers evaluate them on content, originality, and artistic merit. Prizes are NYTTS T-shirts, books, and memberships. Winning posters are exhibited at the annual Turtle and Tortoise Show in June. Some will later be reproduced on T-shirts!

Christmas Seals Kids' Drawing Contest

Ages 6–12; U.S. citizens only
Write: Christmas Seals Kids' Drawing Contest
P.O. Box 25559
Rochester, NY 14625-0559
E-mail: info@lungusa.org
Internet: http://www.christmasseals.org/signup.html
Toll free: 800-LUNG-USA

Thirty million homes receive Christmas Seals adorned with the winning works of art. Few artists receive that kind of exposure!

Your art must be related to the annual theme. For 1996 it was "Feeling Good at the Holidays." Obtain current information from the sponsor.

Create your entry on white, unlined paper measuring eight and a half by eleven inches. Use markers, crayons, or pencils to create a color design. No paint, watercolor, glitter, collage, stickers, photographs, or photocopied content. Your entry must be all your own work—no teaming up with anyone else. Entries are due by the end of March.

Past prizes include a multimedia computer with color printer, and electronic sketch pads.

CyberKids/CyberTeens Contests

Ages 7–12
Write: Mountain Lake Software
298 Fourth Avenue, #401
San Francisco, CA 94118
E-mail: contest@mtlake.com
Internet: http://www.cyberkids.com/
Call: Julie Richer, President
Toll free: 800-669-6574
Main: 415-752-6515
Fax: 415-752-6506

1. CYBERKIDS/CYBERTEENS INTERNATIONAL WRITING AND ART CONTEST

Are you an artist who prefers to draw with a computer mouse instead of crayons or markers? You can in this contest, where you are not only a contestant but also one of the judges. Entries are posted in the pages of this "E-zine." You can check them out at the Web address above and cast your vote. Entries may be created by more than one person, but whoever is listed first will receive the prize and be responsible for sharing it with his or her cocreators.

Fashion your art from traditional materials or on a computer, but the entry must be on paper (no sculptures) no larger than eight and a half by eleven inches.

Deadline for receipt of entries is the end of the year. Voting runs through the middle of March. Prizes have included an Apple Power Macintosh, WACOM graphics tablets, cash, software, and books.

2. CYBERKIDS/CYBERTEENS/CYBERTEACHERS INTERNATIONAL HYPERSTUDIO MULTIMEDIA CONTEST

This contest celebrates computer multimedia, which combines text, graphics, sound, and movement (like video or animation).

Entries may be multimedia presentations of any kind created with HyperStudio, a multimedia authoring program for Windows and Macintosh. If your school doesn't have the HyperStudio software, visit the *Cyberkids* Web site to download a copy that will run for 30 days.

Entries will be judged for good old-fashioned "raw creativity" and impact. Submit yours by mid-December. Finalists will have their entries published on the Internet, and voted on at one of our three major World Wide Web sites.

Dick Blick Linoleum Block Print Contest

Grades 4–6; home schools ineligible
Write: Dick Blick Art Materials
P.O. Box 1267
Galesburg, IL 61402
E-mail: info@dickblick.com
Internet: http://www.dickblick.com/
Call: Advertising Department

Artwork by Vernita Arnold, 5th grade, Farmington, Pennsylvania, the 1997 winner of the Dick Blick Linoleum Block Print Contest. Courtesy of the student artist and Dick Blick Art Materials.

Toll free: 800-447-8192
Main: 309-343-6181
Fax: 309-343-5785

Spattering the kitchen floor with huevos rancheros may be how some folks would merge linoleum and art. But the Dick Blick Art Materials company knows a more appealing way: Carve a piece of linoleum, color it with ink, and make an impression on paper.

Enter prints made from as many different linoleum blocks as you want. Entries are due by the end of April. Prizes include art supplies for your school and a plaque for your wall.

Elvis Art Exhibit and Contest

Up to age 12
Write: Elvis Presley Enterprises
Graceland
3734 Elvis Presley Boulevard
Memphis, TN 38116
Internet: http://www.elvis-presley.com/
Call: Nina Morris or Sheila James
Toll free: 800-238-2010
Main: 901-332-3322
Fax: 901-344-3130

For many music lovers, Elvis Presley will always be the King of Rock and Roll! There's even an Elvis Art Exhibit and Contest each August where faithful fans can pay homage.

Subject matter (no surprise) includes Elvis and his home, Graceland. You can enter the "exhibit only" division (which includes a youth category for ages sixteen and under) that isn't judged. But if you want to compete, enter one of the following divisions: craft (cross-stitch, needlepoint), nonprofessional art (drawing, painting, silk screen, etching, engraving, and sculpture), or photography/computerized media.

Enter by shipping your art to Graceland with an entry form

attached. Deadline is the end of July. You also pay return shipping, unless you donate your masterpiece to Graceland. Art larger than four by four feet may not be exhibited for lack of space. Best of show wins $500.

Federal Junior Duck Stamp Design Contest

Grades K–6
Write: United States Fish and Wildlife Service
Federal Duck Stamp Office
1849 C Street NW
Washington, DC 20240
Internet: http://www.fws.gov/~r9dso/jds/jdhomepg.html
Call: Margaret Wendy, Manager of the Federal Junior Duck
*   Stamp Design and Conservation Program*

Out on a Limb by Ryan McGovern, 11, Ackworth, Georgia, a top-10 national finalist in the Federal Junior Duck Stamp Design Contest. Courtesy of U.S. Fish and Wildlife Service.

Main: 202-208-4354
Direct: 202-208-4369
Fax: 202-208-6296

Money quacks. Just look at the Federal Duck Stamp Program. In 1934 the nation's duck population was getting smaller and smaller. So Congress created the program to raise money to help protect ducks' habitat. Since then, the sale of duck stamps to hunters and collectors has raised $450 million. That money purchased 4.2 million acres of wetlands for national wildlife refuges.

Modeled on that highly successful program, the Junior Duck Stamp Design and Conservation Program in 1990 began promoting conservation through the arts. Teachers and student winners alike praise the curricular program for integrating science and art instruction.

Your entry must be postmarked by February 1. Each state sends its "best of show" artwork to the national competition. The national winning design is reproduced as the year's Federal Junior Duck Stamp, selling for $5. The money goes to conservation education scholarships and awards for the art contest participants.

The top prize is a $2,500 scholarship. The top three national artists, plus one parent and one teacher each, are brought to Washington all expenses paid for an awards ceremony in the fall.

Gutenberg Awards: Student Graphic Arts Contest

Grades 5 and 6
Write: Oakland Technical Center
Southeast Campus
5055 Delemere
Royal Oak, MI 48073
E-mail: Stinnett@mevw.mff.org
Call: Mike Stinnett, Chairman
Main: 810-280-0600, ext. 407
Fax: 810-280-4540

It has taken over 550 years for the world to progress from Johannes Gutenberg's movable-type printing press to word processors and color printers. But one thing hasn't changed: Far from replacing the printed page, electronics give today's graphic artists new power to create eye-catching posters, magazines, books, and newspapers.

To celebrate the achievement of students of the graphic arts, the International Graphic Arts Education Association and the International Association of Printing House Craftsmen sponsor the Gutenberg Awards. There are separate categories for five printing processes.

Entry is free. Deadline is July 1. Top winners receive medals. Industry-provided awards have included graphic arts software.

International Aviation Art Contest

Ages 6–12
Write: National Association of State Aviation Officials
Center for Aviation Research and Education
Metro Place One
8401 Colesville Road, Suite 505
Silver Spring, MD 20910
E-mail: tdwyer or akoranda@nasao.org
Internet: http://www.nasao.org/
Call: Tiffany Dwyer or Amy Koranda, Art Contest Coordinators
Main: 301-495-2848
Fax: 301-585-1803

In 1903 the age of air travel began with a mere twelve-second flight above the dunes of Kitty Hawk, North Carolina. Afterward, Wilbur Wright turned to his brother and said, "Gee, Orville! We've just given mankind wings. Can carry-on luggage and in-flight movies be far behind?"

Okay, that last part didn't happen. Nonetheless, air travel with all its diversions and encumbrances is a routine part of life. This international contest lets you show how you view flying. Your entry must be on paper no larger than eleven and three-quarters inches by sixteen

Artwork by Bryan Church, 8, Cedar Rapids, Iowa, second-place national winner of the 1997 International Aviation Art Contest. Courtesy of NASAO.

and a half inches. Don't use pencil, charcoal, or other nonpermanent media. Crayons, watercolor, acrylic, oil, indelible marker pens, felt-tip pens, and ballpoint pens are fine.

Your best point of contact is your state aviation office. If you can't track it down, contact NASAO, which can send you a flier with details about the contest. You'll still need the address of your state aviation office, because that's where you send your art. Deadline is mid-February.

State winners advance to the national competition. The national winner competes against winners from other countries belonging to the Federation Aeronautique International. International winners receive certificates and medals.

🍎 International Children's Art Exhibition

Grades K–6
Write: Pentel of America

2805 Columbia Street
Torrance, CA 90509
Call: Janet Quan, ICAE Coordinator
Toll free: 800-421-1419
Main: 310-320-3831, ext. 253
Fax: 310-533-0697

Pentel, a Japanese company that manufactures automatic pencils, roller ball pens, ballpoint pens, and art supplies, invites students everywhere to enter the International Children's Art Exhibition (ICAE) contest. In the past quarter century, kids from more than 200 countries have submitted 3 million works of art. The year's best are chosen for different exhibits that tour the globe. It is Pentel's hope that as they see each other's art, kids will realize they have more similarities than differences.

Pick any subject you want, but limit your format to flat, two-dimensional art, such as drawings, paintings, collages, or woodcuts. The judges want to see clear, original images that represent what your country means to you. In 1995, American students submitted more than 3,800 entries and won 1,333 awards.

Your teacher or home-school educator must enter your work, so let them know that you are interested. Your teacher should contact Pentel to be added to the list of rules recipients. Rules are sent during September. Entry deadline is mid-November. All U.S. entries are sent to Tokyo for judging in December. Winners are announced the following May. The U.S. art exhibit makes its first stop at the beginning of September.

KFC/*Family Circle* All American Salute to Mothers

Grades 4–6
Write: KFC/Family Circle Contest Rules
200 East Randolph Street, Suite 6300
Chicago, IL 60601
Call: Alev de Costa

Toll free: 800-874-3273
Main: 312-240-3000
Fax: 312-240-2900

Create the best Mother's Day card, and it will be sold in stores nationwide in time for the annual tribute to moms. The contest begins in October. Submission deadline is early December.

Start with paper that's folded in half, so that it's no larger than five inches wide and eight and a quarter inches tall. Put an illustration on the cover and a message inside. Don't use materials that are difficult to reproduce, such as chalk, sparkles, beads, and lace. Any two-dimensional medium (crayons, paint) is fine.

On a separate sheet, list your name, grade, school, and teacher (or home-school information), home address, and a parent's name and daytime telephone number. A parent or guardian should sign this sheet. Attach it to the back of your Mother's Day card. Entries are due by early December.

Winning cards are chosen from each state and the District of Columbia. The cards are exhibited in New York. The national first-place winner receives $3,500 and a trip with a parent or guardian to the unveiling of the exhibit. Nine other winners receive cash prizes. The top three cards are published in the May issue of *Family Circle*.

Kid's Rainforest Calendar Contest

Grades K–6
Write: Rainforest Action Network
450 Sansome Street, Suite 700
San Francisco, CA 94111
E-mail: rainforest@ran.org
Internet: http://www.ran.org/kids_action/contest.html
Call: Ari Biernoff, Information Coordinator
Main: 415-398-4404
Fax: 415-398-2732

From jaguars and gorillas on the forest floor to monkeys and snakes living in the trees above, the world's rain forests are teeming with life. Sometimes rain forests are referred to as the lungs of the world because they recycle so much carbon dioxide.

Rainforest Action Network works to protect these important lands. It once got a major fast-food company to stop importing beef that had been raised on former rain forest land.

You can help RAN to raise awareness by submitting your rain forest–related art to its annual contest. The contest organizers want "bright, bold, colorful paintings or drawings." But don't use felt-tip pens! Don't submit papier-mâché, sculpture, or other three-dimensional art, either.

Crayons and pencils are fine; pastels and tempera paints are better. The organizers also like collages and cut-and-paste art. Use paper that is eight and a half by eleven inches or eleven by seventeen inches. Instead of leaving a border, color the paper as much as possible.

Ship your artwork flat, not rolled up. Send it in by the deadline at the end of May. Thirteen artworks will be chosen to decorate a calendar that will be distributed around the world. Winning artists are named in the calendar. They also get a free copy. Art for the 1999 calendar was chosen in June 1997.

Lions International Peace Poster

Ages 11 and 12; home schools ineligible
Write: Lions Clubs International
300 Twenty-second Street
Oak Brook, IL 60521-8842
Call: Janet McMahan, Internal Communications Manager
Toll free: 800-288-8846
Main: 630-571-5466, ext. 371
Fax: 630-571-8890

For the winning artist, the long road to victory ends with a trip to New York City to meet the secretary-general at the United Nations.

Building a Peaceful World by Don Nemesio Miranda III, 12, Angono, Rizal, Philippines, the 1996 grand-prize winner of the Lions International Peace Poster. Courtesy of Lions Clubs International.

About 300,000 kids begin the journey by entering their local contest in dozens of countries around the world.

Artists must enter through a local Lions club. If necessary, ask the Oak Brook headquarters (listed above) to match you with a local club. Make this request by the start of October. Local contests conclude at the end of November.

Winning art advances to regional and district- or national-level competitions. The grand-prize winner is chosen from among twenty-four finalists in February.

Little Green Creative Arts Project

Ages 8–12
Write: Sebastian International
Attn: Little Green
6109 DeSoto Avenue
Woodland Hills, CA 91367
Call: Consumer Relations
Toll free: 800-829-7322
Main: 818-999-5112

An all-expense-paid trip for you and a parent to the Costa Rican rain forest is the unique prize offered by this contest. All you do is express your feelings about the environment in writing, art, photography, or song. Your original work should inspire people to recycle and conserve resources. Three winners are chosen in the division for ages eight to eleven and three in the division for ages twelve to fifteen.

The deadline for entering is mid-June. You must be older than seven on that day to be eligible. Entries are judged first in five U.S. regions and one Canadian region. Regional winners advance to the North American final contest in July.

Your first step? Call the toll-free number and ask for a copy of "Planet Power," the flier with the rules and the entry form. You must have the official entry form to enter. No photocopies allowed! Since you can enter as many times as you want, you might as well request a handful of "Planet Power" fliers.

MADD PosterESSAY Contest

Grades 1–6; U.S. citizens only
Write: Mothers Against Drunk Driving

LITTLE GREEN WINNER 1996
Elizabeth Allen, 10 Years Old
Wingdale, NY

Artwork by Elizabeth Allen, 10, Wingdale, New York, 1996 winner of Little Green Creative Arts Project. Courtesy of Sebastian International.

511 East John Carpenter Freeway, Suite 700
Irving, TX 75062
Call: Programs Department
Main: 214-744-6233, ext. 217
Fax: 214-869-2207

Auto crashes are the leading cause of teenage death in the United States, and half of those are alcohol-related. No wonder Mothers Against Drunk Driving (MADD) chose "My World. My Choice. No Alcohol." as the 1997 theme for its PosterESSAY contest.

Each year, local and state contests run from January to March. No contest in your area? Enter the individual competition through the MADD national office. Local contest winners are then entered into a national contest that takes place in March.

National winners are announced in May. Individual and national prizes are awarded. The first-place winner of each grade division wins a $1,000 U.S. Savings Bond, a plaque, and a trip for the winner and a guardian to the awards ceremony in Washington, D.C.

Your poster must be at least twelve by eighteen inches but no larger than eighteen by twenty-four inches. Use crayons, markers, paint, ink, or pencil. Avoid wood, plastic, metal, glass, or breakable materials. Entries must be sturdy for display, so use quality posterboard. Mail your poster flat, not rolled up in a tube.

🍎 Modern Woodmen of America Contests

Write: Modern Woodmen of America
Fraternal Department—Youth Division
1701 First Avenue
Rock Island, IL 61201
Main: 309-786-6481, ext. 7370
Fax: 309-793-5507

These contests may be held in any school in the continental United States by arrangement with an area representative of the MWA, a fraternal insurance company. If you can't find an MWA representative locally, contact the home office (listed above) to be matched with one.

1. NATIONAL ECOLOGY POSTER CONTEST

Grades 3–6

Ecosystems, endangered species, natural resources, and more are covered by the ecology awareness teaching materials available to any classroom at no cost from the MWA.

Classrooms using the materials can participate in the poster contest, which runs from January to November. The theme is always "America the Beautiful." Winners receive a walnut plaque.

2. SAFETY AWARENESS PROGRAM POSTER AWARD

Grades 3–6

Hug a tree if you're lost. Don't seek shelter under a tree during a lightning storm. So what do you do if you're lost in a lightning storm?

Before that happens, learn all about safety from the MWA's Safety Awareness for Youth course. You'll have a chance to win a ribbon for making the best safety poster in your class.

National Character Education Poster Contest

Grades K–6
Write: Character Education Institute
8918 Tesoro Drive, Suite 575
San Antonio, TX 78217-6253
E-mail: cei@CharacterEducation.org
Internet: http://www.CharacterEducation.org/
Call: Barbara Stokes, Office Manager
Toll free: 800-284-0499
Main: 210-829-1727
Fax: 210-829-1729

Every day in the United States, 248 children are arrested for violent crime and 176 kids are arrested for drug abuse. To develop responsible citizens and to help bring these numbers down, some 60,000 classrooms around the world have adopted the Character Education Institute's Character Education Curriculum.

You can enter this contest if your classroom uses the CEC. Usually a teacher sends a class's posters to the institute, but you are welcome to submit yours on your own. Make sure it is no larger than seventeen by twenty-two inches. Don't worry if your art skills are wobbly. The judges will be looking for an original idea that illustrates the values the CEC teaches, like courage, honesty, and justice.

Deadline for entry is March 1. Top prize in each of the three grade divisions is $25.

National Garden Week Poster Contest

Ages 5–12
Write: National Garden Week Poster Contest
Attn: Cindy Waldman
National Junior Horticulture Association
5759 Sandalwood NE
North Canton, OH 44721
Call: Cindy Waldman
Main: 330-492-3252

You'll get a packet of seeds just for entering this contest, and if you win, you'll also get a set of garden tools and a $10 seed gift certificate.

To be eligible, you must join NJHA's Young America division. Membership is free. Just fill out a form, send it in, and you're a member.

Your "poster" should be on an ordinary sheet of typing or computer paper. Your color artwork must include the annual theme somewhere. For the 1996 contest, the theme was "With a Touch of Love, Everything Can Grow."

Enter only once. Deadline for receipt of entries is December 1. Enclose an SASE if you want to learn the results.

National School Traffic Safety Poster Program

Grades K–6
Write: American Automobile Association

Artwork by the 1996 Elementary Grand Award Winner of the National School Traffic Safety Poster Program, 11, Brooklyn, New York. Courtesy of AAA.

National Poster Program headquarters
1000 AAA Drive
Heathrow, FL 32746-5063
Call: Vicki Powers, Manager, Education Programs
Direct: 407-444-7912
Fax: 407-444-7956

AAA's annual poster contest makes thousands of kids aware of traffic safety as they illustrate one of up to twenty slogans for the year, such as "Cooperate with Your Safety Patrol" and "Curb the Urge to Dash Across."

The submission deadline falls at the beginning of February. Posters are judged on originality, technique, visual impact, and message as it relates to traffic safety practice.

State and national winners receive U.S. Savings Bonds. AAA distributes millions of copies of the art that wins the grand prize.

National Women's Hall of Fame Poster Contest

Grades 4–6
Write: National Women's Hall of Fame
P.O. Box 335
Seneca Falls, NY 13148
Call: Mary Gratton, Operations Manager
Main: 315-568-8060
Fax: 315-568-2976

American women have distinguished themselves since colonial days, when Betsy Ross designed our nation's flag. Two centuries later, that flag was part of the uniform worn by Sally Ride, the first American woman in space. If you have ever drawn inspiration from a famous American female of the past or present, share it in this contest.

Poster entries interpret the theme chosen for each year's National Women's History Month (March). Deadline is the end of that month. Winners are notified in May. Top prize is $100.

NRA Youth Wildlife Art Contest

Grades 1–6
Write: National Rifle Association
11250 Waples Mill Road
Fairfax, VA 22030
Internet: http://www.nra.org/
Call: NRA Community Service Programs Division
Toll free: 800-672-3888

A Grizzly Portrait by Melissa Chellette, 12, Natchitoches, Louisiana, 1996 winner of the NRA Youth Wildlife Art Contest. Courtesy of the artist.

Main: 703-267-1000
Direct: 703-267-1595
Fax: 703-267-3993

The animal your art shows must be one that can be hunted or trapped legally in North America: deer, bears, pheasants, squirrels, rabbits, quail, ducks, geese, and so on. Nongame or endangered animals, such as eagles and snakes, are excluded.

Deadline for entry falls around the start of November. First-place winners receive $300. Winning artwork is published in the January issue of *InSights,* an NRA magazine for its younger members.

🍎 Ocean Pals™ National Student Poster Contest

Grades K–6
Write: Beneath the Sea, Inc.
495 New Rochelle Road
Bronxville, NY 10708
Main: 914-664-4310
Fax: 914-664-4315

Now here's a (sea)worthy cause. Share your awareness and concern for the marine environment by entering this contest. Create a fish-friendly poster based on the annual theme. In 1996–97, the theme was sea creatures that camouflage themselves and what we can do to protect their environment. For current information, write to the Bronxville address. Don't expect to hear anything before autumn.

Only one artist per poster is allowed. Make it eighteen by twenty-four inches, with a one-inch border. Pen, pencil, colored pencils, markers, crayons, watercolors, and acrylic paints are okay. But forget about charcoal, oil paints, pastels, chalk, glitter, or sand.

Schools select their best three posters to send to the regional competition. Note which states belong in which region:

★   **Southeast.** Florida only. Write: Ocean Pals Contest, Sonia Smith, FSDA/Ocean Expo, 636 Forty-first Avenue NE, St. Petersburg, FL 33703.

★   **West.** Alaska, California, Hawaii, Oregon, and Washington. Write: Ocean Pals Contest, Carol Rose, Underwater Society of America, P.O. Box 628, Daly City, CA 94017.

★   **East.** The other forty-four states. Write: Ocean Pals Contest, Leesa Hernandez, 483 Oscawana Lake Road, Putnam Valley, NY 10579.

Postmark deadline is mid-December. Posters must be unmounted, mailed flat, with a contest entry form attached to the back. National winners are notified in February. Prizes are medals and U.S. Savings Bonds.

Project Environment Essay and Poster Contest

Grades 4–6
Write: California Table Grape Commission
P.O. Box 27320
Fresno, CA 93729-7320
Call: Cara Peracchi-Douglas, Director of Communications
Main: 209-447-8350
Fax: 209-447-9184

Hold on! This contest was discontinued by the California Table Grape Commission. But don't get a case of sour grapes—they plan to hold a new contest. Details will be available in the fall of 1997, either from your school's food service director or by writing directly to the CTGC. Prizes in the old contest included U.S. Savings Bonds, mountain bikes, and camping gear.

Read Writing and Art Awards

Grade 6; U.S. citizens only
Write: **Read Magazine**
The Weekly Reader Corporation
P.O. Box 120023
Stamford, CT 06912-0023
E-mail: kdavis@weeklyreader.com
Internet: http://www.weeklyreader.com/
Call: Kate Davis, Associate Editor
Main: 203-705-3500
Fax: 860-346-5826

Create the best cover artwork, and it will appear on the cover of *Read*'s annual student issue in May.

There's no theme. Draw or paint whatever you want. Vertical formats work best because they fit on the magazine cover; *Read* will shrink the art to fit if necessary. Don't bother with any text or title; the magazine staff will add that. Be original and colorful. Use any medium, as long as the finished product is two-dimensional.

Enter by mid-December. Top prize is $100 and publication. Most participants are in junior high or high school, but the editors would love to get more submissions from sixth graders.

🍎 Reflections Program

Grades pre-K–6; home-school eligibility varies locally
Write: National PTA
330 North Wabash Avenue, Suite 2100
Chicago, IL 60611-3690
Internet: http://www.pta.org/
Call: Arts and Education Program Coordinator
Main: 312-670-6782, ext. 352
Fax: 312-670-6783

The National PTA is the largest child advocacy program in the country. Its Reflections Program stimulates students to express themselves through various "art areas": literature, photography, visual arts, and musical composition. You'll have to stick to the year's theme, but it tends to be pretty open. "Dare to Discover . . ." and "Imagine That . . ." were themes in previous years.

Rules and deadlines vary from state to state, so give your local PTA or PTSA a jingle. Local chapters decide whether home-schooled kids can participate in the Reflections Program.

You have to win your local, district, and state competitions to reach the national level of judging. Place and honorable mention awards are given for each arts area and grade division. One Outstanding Interpretation is chosen from all the placing entries in each arts area based on the most creative interpretation of the theme.

Prizes vary from year to year. A traveling exhibit showcases all the national place and honorable mention works.

SSIP Intergalactic Art Competition

Grades 3–6
Write: National Science Teachers Association
Attn: SSIP
1840 Wilson Boulevard
Arlington, VA 22201-3000
E-mail: ssip@nsta.org
Internet: http://www.nsta.org/
Call: Kathlyn Berry, SSIP Director
Main: 703-243-7100
Fax: 703-243-7177

Saturn's rings glow faintly in your rearview scanner. Invisible ahead is good ole planet Earth. Zooming past Callisto, one of Jupiter's largest moons, you are suddenly riveted by the sight of . . .

You fill in the rest of the details. But do it with your paintbrush, crayon, pencil, pastels, or computer graphics software. Then enter the result in the Space Science Student Involvement Program (SSIP) Intergalactic Art Competition. You could win a trip to NASA's Space Camp!

Anything in space, known or unknown, can be your topic: planets, moons, asteroids, meteoroids, comets, nebulae, and so forth. Enter as an individual, do your own work, and don't use copyrighted materials, such as characters from *Star Trek*.

There are many more rules, and they must be followed to the letter, so send off for the brochure by September. Your entry must be postmarked early the following January.

Your national first-place art is a ticket to Space Camp for you, and to the National Space Science Symposium for you and a teacher. There are prizes, too, for top winners at the state level. National and state winning art becomes part of a touring exhibit.

The UNICEF "Kids Helping Kids" Greeting Card Contest

Up to age 12
Write: Pier 1 Imports
Attn: Joy Rich
P.O. Box 961020
Fort Worth, TX 76161
E-mail: public_relations@pier1.com
Internet: http://www.pier1.com/
Call: Joy Rich, Public Relations
Toll free: 800-245-4595
Main: 817-878-8000
Direct: 817-878-8345
Fax: 817-878-7860

Create the best illustration on a holiday season greeting card, and you and two family members will be brought to New York for an awards reception held at the United Nations. The 1997 theme is "Kids Helping Kids."

Artwork by Adam Yukio Toda, 12, Los Angeles, California, 1996 winner of the UNICEF "Kids Helping Kids" Greeting Card Contest. Courtesy of Pier 1 Imports.

Pick up an entry form containing the year's theme and rules at a Pier 1 Imports store in September. To locate the nearest Pier 1 or get the entry packet by mail, call the toll-free number. Your entry must be submitted between September and mid-October. Award winners are announced in early November and honored the following month at the UN.

The two winning designs from the ages-eight-to-thirteen division and the seven-and-under division become UNICEF greeting cards sold only at Pier 1 during the following year's holiday season. Sales of UNICEF greeting cards by Pier 1 since 1985 have raised $7 million for the children's relief agency.

See also:

HOMETOWN TREES KIDS ART CONTEST (chapter 6, under section "Multidiscipline Competitions")

NEWSCURRENTS STUDENT EDITORIAL CARTOON CONTEST (chapter 2, under section "Journalism")

YOUTH HONOR AWARDS (chapter 3, under section "Fiction")

Dance and Music

BMI Student Composer Awards

Up to age 12
Write: BMI Student Composer Awards
320 West Fifty-seventh Street
New York, NY 10019

This contest was established in 1951 to encourage young composers. Prizes total $16,000, including the top prize of $3,000.

Your composition can be of any style and length. The judges value "vital musicality and clarity of expression" over "academic finesse." The composition can have lyrics. Music with ordinary scoring should be submitted on score paper. Electronic music and tapes of graphic works, which cannot be adequately presented in score form, may be substituted on cassette.

Entries are due by early February. Awards are announced by the end of June.

🍎Keyboard Teachers Association International Contests

All ages
Write: Keyboard Teachers Association International
361 Pin Oak Lane
Westbury, NY 11590-1941
Internet: http://www.516web.com/music/ktai/
Call: Albert DeVito, President
Main: 516-333-3236

Here are some events to reward you for all those hours of practice and theory. For you to participate, your teacher must be a member of the Keyboard Teachers Association International. Get yours to join, if necessary. Membership costs $25 a year.

KTAI holds a student evaluation program each spring for students at all levels of ability. Participation costs $10. You choose what music to perform, from baroque to contemporary. You must also play some required exercises, such as scales and arpeggios. Your teacher records your performance and sends the tape to "helpful and understanding" KTAI evaluators. All participants receive an evaluation report and Certificate of Achievement.

KTAI also holds an annual musical composition contest. Submit a tape and a written score by April 1. (The deadline never changes.) Entry fee is $10 per composition.

Although there are cash awards of $500, no students have entered this contest in the past two years. But the contest will definitely continue, Albert DeVito says. It's up to teachers to encourage students to participate.

🍎 Music Teachers National Association Composition Competition

Grades 1–6
Write: Music Teachers National Association
441 Vine Street, Suite 505
Cincinnati, OH 45202-2814
E-mail: MTNAadmin@aol.com
Internet: http://www.mtna.com/
Main: 513-421-1420
Fax: 513-421-2503

Did you compose an interesting tune while testing the music software that came with your home computer? Maybe you should submit it to this contest. About a quarter of students who enter do make use of their computer.

You can enter if you take music lessons from a teacher who is an

MTNA member. Urge yours to join, if necessary. (National dues are $40. There are also state and possibly local dues.) You will submit a printout of the musical score and a tape recording of a performance. You need not be the performer; in some cases the judges will even accept a recording of your computer playing the music. Length must not exceed ten minutes.

In 1996 more than seventy elementary school students participated. The winning composition was a duet for piano fourhand (that's two people playing one piano) of three to four minutes. The national coordinator for the contest says the compositions can be surprisingly sophisticated; he sometimes tells his college students that he wished they composed that well!

Don't let that deter you, though. All students who enter their state competitions benefit from the judge's feedback.

The deadlines to enter your state contest could range from the start of September to October. Entry fees vary by state, too. The June/July issue of *American Music Teacher* magazine contains rules and deadline information, but doesn't mention entry fees. Ask your state organization about those. First prize is $300.

National Federation of Music Club Awards

Write: National Federation of Music Clubs
1336 North Delaware Street
Indianapolis, IN 46202
Main: 317-638-4003
Fax: 317-638-0503

NFMC publishes a ten-page chart, available for $1, that describes its contests and awards. The following lists only those events open to students up to age twelve. Students perform live for some events and submit a tape for others.

1. ANNUAL MUSIC CONTESTS

Stillman-Kelley Scholarship (instrumentalists): up to age twelve; apply by February 1; first place, $1,000.

NFMC Thelma Byrum Piano Award (piano): up to age twelve; apply by February 1; first place, $300.

NFMC Wendell Irish Viola Award (viola): age twelve as of March 1 of year of auditions; apply by February 1; four awards of $700.

NFMC Junior Festival (instrumentalists and vocalists): up to age twelve; deadline and prizes are not listed.

NFMC Junior Composers Contest: up to age twelve; apply by February 1; prizes up to $100.

NFMC Music for the Blind Award (blind composition); ages ten to twelve; apply by March 1; first place, $100.

NFMC Music for the Blind Performance Awards (blind instrumentalists and vocalists): up to age twelve; apply by March 1; eight awards of $200.

NFMC W. Paul Benzinger Memorial Award Music for the Blind Performance (blind instrumentalists and vocalists): up to age twelve; apply by March 1; four awards of $200.

NFMC Joyce Walsh Junior Scholarship for the Handicapped (handicapped instrumentalists and vocalists): age twelve; apply by February 1; first place, $1,000.

2. DANCE

Age 12

Yes, NFMC does award money for something besides music—namely, dance. There are Annual Junior Awards in the categories of ballet and theater dance. You must have reached your twelfth birthday by March 1 of the year of auditions. Apply by April 1. Entry fee is $5. Prizes range up to $150.

3. SUMMER MUSIC SCHOLARSHIPS

Eastern Music Festival (orchestral instruments and voice): age twelve; apply by April 1; scholarship of $300.

Meadowmount School (violin, viola, or cello): ages ten to twelve; apply by April 1; two scholarships of $300.

The Walden School (composition and theoretical skills): ages nine to twelve; apply by April 1; scholarship of $400.

Panasonic Young Soloists Award

Up to age 12
Write: Very Special Arts
John F. Kennedy Center for the Performing Arts
1300 Connecticut Avenue NW, Suite 700
Washington, DC 20036
E-mail: elenaw@vsarts.org
Internet: http://www.vsarts.org
Call: Elena Widder, Assistant Director
Toll free: 800-933-8721
Main: 202-628-2800
Fax: 202-737-0725
TDD: 202-737-0645

Every year, the Very Special Arts Young Soloists Program recognizes outstanding young musicians with disabilities. Recipients exhibit exceptional talent as vocalists or instrumentalists. Musicians submit tapes of their work by mail before the November 1 deadline. Four are chosen to receive the scholarship award of $5,000.

See also:
LITTLE GREEN CREATIVE ARTS PROJECT (this chapter, under section "Art")
REFLECTIONS PROGRAM (this chapter, under section "Art")

Film/Video

International Student Media Festival

Grades K–6
Write: Ann Arundel County Public Schools

Attn: Michael Maszczenski
2644 Riva Road
Annapolis, MD 21401
E-mail: michaelm@umd5.umd.edu
Call: Michael Maszczenski
Main: 410-222-5263
Direct: 410-222-5265
Home: 410-643-5666
Fax: 410-222-5601

Remember the movie *Jurassic Park*? Some of its animation was the work of Dave Masters, a former winner at the International Student Media Festival who now works for Walt Disney Company. See where entering contests can lead?

Ask the organizers if your state currently participates in this contest. If not, the problem may be lack of an adult coordinator. In that case, ask your parent, teacher, or another adult you know to be the coordinator.

Next, get busy on your media project. You can enter alone or as part of a group, class, or club. Often the entries at the elementary-school level are class projects of five to thirty students. In fact, because they do usually enter as a team, elementary school kids account for at least as much participation in this contest as older students.

Kids from all schools, not just wealthy ones, find a way to enter. "Sometime schools don't have the equipment, but the parents do," Michael Maszczenski says.

Your entry probably will belong in the sequential stills category. That kind of entry is fairly easy to create. It resembles a slide show or film strip, and might have music or narration. Maszczenski predicts that elementary school kids will soon start using powerful and easy-to-use computer software to create more challenging entries, such as animation, multimedia, and live-action video.

All entries must be in VHS format. Keep the running time, including credits, under seven minutes. Don't enter the same work in more than one category, or you'll be disqualified!

Entries must be in the mail at the start of October. Enclose a $10 fee. Send a postcard to be added to the mailing list. You'll get two updates a year about the contest.

Excerpts from the winning entries are shown during the annual convention of the Association for Educational Communications and Technology (AECT) in February.

International Wildlife Film Festival/Photography Contest

Write: 802 East Front Street
Missoula, MT 59802
E-mail: iwff@montana.com
Internet: http://www.montana.com/iwff
Call: Dr. Charles Jonkel, Festival Director
Main: 406-728-9380
Fax: 406-728-2881

1. INTERNATIONAL WILDLIFE FILM FESTIVAL

Ages 3–12

Until recently, wildlife films tended to make animals seem either fierce and dangerous like lions or cute and cuddly like baby seals. Neither image is a complete picture. To encourage more realistic portrayals of animals, famous bear biologist Charles Jonkel founded what is now the world's longest-running wildlife film competition and festival. It emphasizes wildlife films that are accurate and educational as well as artistic and entertaining.

One of the sixteen categories is School Group. Despite the name, you can enter a film that you created alone, without any school connection. Enter the division for ages three to twelve. The organizers say they get numerous entries from young students and would like even more. Just make sure your parents know about it before you poke your camera into a mountain lion's den! Better yet, choose an animal that isn't dangerous as your subject.

Enter by early February. Your film or video must have been created during the previous calendar year. The entry fee for the School Group category is $25. Requests for a waiver are considered case by case.

Winners are notified in advance of the April festival so they can make plans to attend. Prizes are plaques shaped like Montana. More important is the honor that comes from doing well at this world-famous event.

2. IWFF WILDLIFE PHOTOGRAPHY CONTEST

All ages

This contest has divisions for two types of photographers: those who earn more than $1,000 a year from photography, and those who earn less. You'll compete in the second group, which is sure to include some highly skilled adult photographers for whom picture taking is a serious hobby.

The judges look for artistic portrayals of wildlife. Submit a color or black-and-white print that is eight by ten inches or larger. It should be matted and ready to display, with hanger attached. However, do not use a frame or glass.

Deadline is early March. Entry fee is $7 per photo, with no limit on submissions. Put your name, address, telephone number, and a photo title on the back. Indicate where your photo was taken, especially if at a zoo or game farm. If you want to sell your photo, put a price on the back. If someone attending the April exhibit buys your photo, IWFF will keep a 30-percent commission. Unsold photos may be picked up in late May. Photos submitted with a return mailer and postage are sent back by late June.

MBG Video Contest

Grades 1–6
Write: MBG Learning Network
2025 South Brentwood Boulevard
St. Louis, MO 63144

E-mail: evrgreen@icon-stl.net
Internet: http://cissus.mobot.org/MBGnet
Call: Bettie Schwartz, Project Director
Toll free: 800-927-9229
Home: 314-997-0065
Fax: 314-968-1572

MBG (Missouri Botanical Gardens) Learning Network documents the world's different natural environments using five-minute videos from individual students or class projects. To encourage participation, MBG sponsors occasional contests with specific environments in mind. First was the desert, the forest, and the grasslands. Next came the rain forest and arctic landscapes.

Most recently the topic was aquatic: swamps, large rivers, the Great Lakes, and so on. Grand prize was $100 cash and $200 worth of MBG products for the winners' classroom. Information about the winning videos and their producers is posted on the MBG Learning Network Online.

"We have received video footage from all around the world which is incorporated in our newest shows," Project Director Bettie Schwartz says. "We will be repeating the student video contest idea with different subjects as they come up. We will also be working on an environmental project with middle school students, too." Check the Web site for the latest.

Sinking Creek Film Celebration

Grades K–6
Write: Sinking Creek
Vanderbilt University
402 Sarratt Student Center
Nashville, TN 37240
E-mail: creek@ctrvax.vanderbilt.edu
Call: Michael Catalano, Artistic Director
Main: 615-343-3419
Direct: 615-322-4234
Fax: 615-343-9461

You might know Nashville as the home of the Grand Old Opry, guitar-shaped swimming pools, and more country-western recording labels than an Elvis impersonator has rhinestones.

But that's just one side of Music City. There's also Vanderbilt University and its annual film festival. You enter the Young Film/Video Maker division, which has a category for "high school or younger" students. Don't be afraid of being the youngest competitor. Just submit the best film you can. The judges care about the quality of the film, not the age of the student.

Separately judged genres include animation, documentary, experimental, dramatic, music video, and mixed genre. Inquire about deadlines. Entry fees vary by running time, from $25 for 20 minutes to $55 for 120 minutes. Foreign or late entries each add $5. Films should be submitted on video for prescreening.

Winning entries are showcased at the festival the following November. Numerous cash prizes are awarded, including $1,500 for best of show.

Weekly Reader/Panasonic Video Voyages Contest

Grades 4–6
Write: **Weekly Reader**
Video Voyages Contest
P.O. Box 120023
Stamford, CT 06912-0023
E-mail: llewis@weeklyreader.com
Internet: http://www.weeklyreader.com
Call: Lois Lewis, Associate Editor
Main: 203-705-3500

Calling all future Hollywood directors and TV journalists! Show how talented you already are by entering the best video in this contest.

Form a team with some classmates to create one video of up to ten minutes. Choose your topic from among these categories:

★   **Personal.** An important time in the life of a team member, a dream, a memory, something imagined. It could even be a music video.

★   **Local.** An issue or bit of history from your community. Make a minidocumentary about a local resident.

★   **National.** Issues of importance to all Americans.

★   **Historical.** An enactment from the life of a famous person or of a famous event.

★   **Future.** A science fiction or fantasy journey.

Really want to win? Blow away the judges with your creativity, originality, and production skills. "And we like to laugh," the judges say. Plan ahead, prepare carefully, and polish the final product. And don't forget to submit your entry by mid-March.

Prizes go to the students' schools. The top award is a Panasonic camcorder, VCR, TV, and T-shirts for the whole team.

Photography

Note: You do not have to develop your own film in order to enter these contests. Just take a great picture and let a photo lab do the rest.

Camera Bug International

All ages
Write: Camera Bug World Headquarters
2106 Hoffnagle Street
Philadelphia, PA 19152
Call: Leonard Friedman, Director
Main: 215-742-5515
Fax: 215-925-5508

This contest is for people who take pictures for fun, not for a living. Any subject and format are allowed. Entry fee is $5 per photo. All contestants receive a booklet on basic tips for photo competitions. Prizes are Camera Bag merchandise. Send an SASE for contest guidelines and entry forms.

Kodak International Newspaper Snapshot Awards

All ages
Write: Kodak Consumer Imaging
343 State Street
Rochester, NY 14650
Internet: http://www.kodak.com/
Call: Jim Franklin, KINSA Coordinator
Toll free: 800-242-2424

For you to enter, your local newspaper must participate. Around 150 U.S. and 50 foreign newspapers do each year. If yours doesn't, get your friends to help you write letters asking the newspaper to take part.

Participating newspapers select winning images in a six-week competition every fall. Those are forwarded to Kodak for further judging. You must use Kodak film and paper. If you're a winner, you must give Kodak the right to use your photo for at least five years.

The grand prize is $10,000. Prizes total $50,000. Understandably, this is a very popular contest. Enter your single best image and hope for the best!

National Wildlife Photo Contest

All ages
Write: National Wildlife
Drawer C-97

8925 Leesburg Pike
Vienna, VA 22184

You mean you're not a professional photographer? No problem. This contest is open to amateurs, too. Categories are wildlife, landscapes, humor in nature, people in nature, plant life, and underwater. Submit up to five photos. Deadline is early June. Prizes total $6,000. Winning photos and rules for the next contest are published in the December/ January issue of *National Wildlife* magazine.

See also:

AMERICAN MORGAN HORSE ASSOCIATION CONTESTS (this chapter, under section "Art")

ELVIS ART EXHIBIT AND CONTEST (this chapter, under section "Art")

INTERNATIONAL WILDLIFE FILM FESTIVAL/ PHOTOGRAPHY CONTEST (this chapter, under section "Film/Video")

LITTLE GREEN CREATIVE ARTS PROJECT (this chapter, under section "Art")

REFLECTIONS PROGRAM (this chapter, under section "Art")

2

Headliners

Essay, Journalism, and Speech

What's happening? What's on your mind? Here are some opportunities to let us know. Essay and speech contests give you a topic. You tell us why that topic matters. Think of it as dancing to someone else's tune—but you get to make up the dance!

Journalism contests might let you air your opinions on your own favorite topic, if the category is editorial or editorial cartoon. If the category is newswriting, the judges only want straight facts about the explosive events of the day—no opinions allowed! From the contests in this chapter, choose the ones that give you your say, your way!

Essay

AMHAY Literary Contest

Up to age 12

Write: American Morgan Horse Association (See page 1 for contact and other information about the contests.)

If you like to write about horses, this contest will put you in the saddle. The original Justin Morgan horse, described as having "tremendous endurance and a delicate head," was the only horse to sire a distinctive breed in the United States. Display your affection for the Morgan through your writing.

Check with AMHA for the current year's theme and official entry form. Past themes included "Olympic-Size Morgan Dreams" and "If My Morgan Could Talk." Your essay of under 1,000 words must be postmarked by the start of October. Top prize is $25.

ByLine Student Contests

Grades 1–6
Write: Student Page Contests
ByLine
P.O. Box 130596
Edmond, OK 73013-0001
Internet: http://www.bylinemag.com/
Call: Marcia Preston, Editor-Publisher
Main: 405-348-5591

Every September *ByLine,* a magazine for working writers, announces its monthly creative writing contests for students for the remainder of the school year. One month the editors want a personal essay, the next a poem, after that a short story, and so on. Entry fee is $1. Students may enter the contests whether or not their schools subscribe to *ByLine.* (The subscription price is $20 for eleven issues.) Your teacher must verify that your entry is original work.

ByLine publishes winning entries. The writers are awarded up to $25, plus a copy of the issue in which their work appears.

Creating a Better World Internet Essay Contest

Up to age 12
Write: Creating a Better World Contest

The Way to Happiness Foundation
P.O. Box 2930
Hollywood, CA 90028
E-mail: twthfoundation@thewaytohappiness.org
Internet: http://www.able.org/youthess/betterwo.htm
Call: Essay Competition Director
Main: 213-962-7906
Fax: 213-962-9605

This contest is based on the book *The Way to Happiness* by L. Ron Hubbard. He is remembered as a major science fiction author and founder of the Church of Scientology, but *The Way to Happiness* is neither fiction nor specifically religious. With chapters like "Be Worthy of Trust" and "Love and Help Children," the book promotes morals and values. The foundation promotes the book.

There are five age divisions for eighteen and under for the essay contest. Teachers are encouraged to involve their classrooms, but students may enter individually. Essays should be 100 to no more than 400 words. They should be based on part or all of the book. The foundation will provide copies of *The Way to Happiness* for $10 per dozen, plus $4 shipping and handling.

The contest is held in the fall and again in the spring. Enter by mail or E-mail. There are sixty-two prizes of $100 and numerous other prizes. In fact, everyone who enters gets a prize, the organizers say.

🍎 Creative Writing Essay Contest

Grades 5–6
Write: Modern Woodmen of America (*See page 21 for contact and other information about the contest.*)

This contest promotes clear writing. It may be held in any school in the continental United States by arrangement with an area representative of the MWA, a fraternal insurance company. If you can't find an

MWA representative locally, contact the home office (listed on page 21) to be matched with one.

MWA provides brochures for students that explain the contest and show the trophies and ribbons they can win. Each essay includes up to 500 words. The 1996–97 topic was "A New Horizon." Although you are given a topic, you are expected to use lots of imagination. Your essay can be as full of fiction as a short story, as long as you stick to the topic.

A minimum of twelve students per school must participate. MWA says the contest is most successful when teachers make it part of class work for English or writing. Schools hold the contest anytime between September and June. However, they must register with the MWA at least thirty days before the contest date to ensure that they get the trophies in time for the contest. The top three winners in each school receive a solid walnut trophy. The school also gets a trophy, on which the winners' names are engraved.

Firearms Civil Rights Legal Defense Fund Essay Contest

Grades 1–6
Write: FCRLDF Essay Desk
11250 Waples Mill Road
Fairfax, VA 22030-7400
Internet: http://www.nra.org/
Toll free: 800-672-3888
Main: 703-267-1560

What is the Second Amendment, and why is it important to our country? That's the general idea you will address in this essay contest.

Write in January to get the specific theme of the year's contest. Essays should be about 1,000 words. Postmark deadline is July 4. Prizes are U.S. Savings Bonds worth $1,000, $600, $200, and $100.

Grandmother Earth National Writing Contest

Grades K–6
Write: Grandmother Earth
8463 Deerfield Lane
Germantown, TN 38138
Call: Frances Cowden, GEC Contest Chairperson
Main: 901-758-0804
Fax: 901-757-0506

Even if it's already been published, your prose of 1,000 words or fewer or your poem of fifty lines or fewer may be entered in this contest. And nonwinning work as well as prizewinners may be published in Grandmother Earth anthologies. Environmental issues and human values are the themes.

Entry fee is $10 for up to three works, and $2 for each additional. The deadline falls in July. All entrants receive a copy of that year's Grandmother Earth anthology. Prizes vary each year.

There is no entry fee for *A Child's View,* an anthology of art and poetry on topics of concern to children. That deadline falls in May. Submissions must be original work. There are some $25 merit awards. Otherwise, students receive a copy of the anthology.

Letters About Literature

Grade 6; U.S. citizens only
Write: Read Magazine
The Weekly Reader Corporation
P.O. Box 120023
Stamford, CT 06912-0023
Internet: http://www.weeklyreader.com/
Call: Editor, Read Magazine

Have you read a book lately that really made a big impression on you—maybe even changed the way you think about yourself and the world? Tell how in a letter that you submit to *Read*. You and a parent or guardian could win a week in Washington, D.C.!

Pick a book that you read recently, one that really gave you strong emotions. Then write up to 1,000 words to the author explaining what the book taught you about yourself. No need to repeat the plot. Just explain what one of the events or characters had in common with you or your life. Keep your letter honest, personal, and conversational, as if you're talking to the author.

Send your letter with the official entry form to *Read* by early December. (*Do not* send anything to the author.) The winning entries will appear in *Read*.

Dear Mr. Richard Wright,

   Black Boy had a great effect on me. Before I read this book, I considered myself a very unemotional person. I thought nothing could make me cry. As I got more and more into the book, I began to feel very sad. When I got to the part where you and your brother had no food to eat and y'all daddy had left, I felt horrified. I thought to myself How could someone do that to their children? I used to ask my mother that same question about my daddy. You see, like your daddy, my daddy was the breadwinner in our family. But he never cared what happened to me and my siblings one way or the other . . .

Excerpt from letter by 1995 cowinner Ayesha Henderson, Plaquemine, Louisiana. Special permission granted, published, and copyrighted © 1996 by Weekly Reader Corporation. All Rights Reserved.

MADD PosterESSAY Contest

Grades 1–6; U.S. citizens only

Write: Mothers Against Drunk Driving (See page 19 for contact and other information about the contest.)

Each year, Mothers Against Drunk Driving (MADD) sponsors local and state contests run from January to March. No contest in your area? Enter the individual competition through the MADD national office. Local contest winners are then entered into a national contest that takes place in March.

National winners are announced in May. Individual and national prizes are awarded. The first-place winner of each grade division wins a $1,000 U.S. Savings Bond, plaque, and a trip for the winner and a guardian to the awards ceremony in Washington, D.C.

Write 250 words. Poetry isn't acceptable. If you prefer, your entry can be in Spanish. Typed entries are preferred, but neat printing in black ink is fine as long as it's readable.

National Americanism Essay Contest

Grade 6
*Write: **AMVETS** (See page 3 for contact and other information about the contest.)*

AMVETS is an organization of veterans and current members of the U.S. armed forces. It promotes veterans' issues and the American way of life. The theme of this contest changes annually. For 1996, the theme was "What Does an American Veteran Mean to Me?"

Submit an essay in your handwriting of up to 250 words. National prizes are U.S. Savings Bonds of $1,000, $750, and $500. The first-place winner also receives a plaque.

National Association for Bilingual Education Contest

Grades 1–6; home schools ineligible
Write: National Association for Bilingual Education
c/o Jaime de la Isla

Houston Independent School District
3830 Richmond Avenue
Houston, TX 77036
Call: Jaime de la Isla, National Coordinator
Main: 713-892-6800
Direct: 713-892-6816
Fax: 713-892-7859

Are you enrolled in a bilingual program at school that you think is really great? NABE started this contest in 1981 to prove that students enrolled in bilingual education programs do, in fact, learn English.

Public school students enrolled in bilingual education programs write an essay—in English—on a theme related to bilingual education or bilingualism. Among the 2,000 or so students who enter annually, Hispanics in the U.S. Southwest are heavily represented. But previous winners have also been Native Americans or Vietnamese immigrants living in Alaska, Montana, and Louisiana.

There are separate divisions for elementary, middle, and high school. Eligible students write between 150 and 500 words about being bilingual and its impact on their life. Deadline comes in late spring. Obtain current details from the bilingual or English-as-a-Second-Language (ESL) teacher at your school, or from the NABE national office.

Three winners per division receive cash scholarships and other prizes.

National Women's Hall of Fame Essay Contest

Grades 4–6
Write: *National Women's Hall of Fame* (*See page 25 for contact and other information about the contest.*)

Each year a new theme is chosen for National Women's History Month (March). Write an essay about the theme and submit it by the end of that month. Winners are notified in May. Top prize is $100.

Paul A. Witty Outstanding Literature Award

Grades K–6
Write: International Reading Association
Attn: Dr. Cathy Collins Block
Texas Christian University
TCU Box 287900
Fort Worth, TX 76129
E-mail: cblock@gamma.is.tcu.edu
Call: Dr. Cathy Collins Block, Professor of Education
Main: 817-921-7000, ext. 6789
Fax: 817-921-7701

Beauty of expression, originality, and creativity—why, that sounds just like your style of writing. Submit a sample and you might win the Paul A. Witty Outstanding Literature Award. Witty was a professor of education who helped found the International Reading Association, a group of 50,000 teachers of elementary-level reading or high school English.

You may submit up to five poems or a single work of prose (short story, essay, or even a play) of around 1,000 words.

Postmark deadline is always February 1. Winners will be determined by mid-March, with the awards of at least $25 made at the IRA annual convention in late April or early May.

Read Writing and Art Awards

Grade 6; U.S. citizens only
Write: Read Magazine (*See page 29 for contact and other information about the contest.*)

"I had a farm in Africa . . ." began Karen Blixen in her famous memoir that became the movie *Out of Africa,* with Robert Redford and Meryl Streep. Did you ever have an experience that a Hollywood star would want to re-create? Maybe you did, but don't realize it. A good narrative or story tells more than just what happened. It reveals the meaning behind the events, leaving us with a new way of looking at things.

Your essay of up to five double-spaced pages should also be a first-person account ("I did this. I saw that.") of something that really happened to you. Reveal your observations, memories, and feelings. Relate the incident to an important issue like honesty or loyalty, but keep things exciting. Don't sound like a preacher or politician. Let readers feel what you feel.

Enter by mid-December. Top prize is $100 and inclusion in the May student issue of *Read*. The editors would love to get more submissions from sixth graders.

Vegetarian Resource Group's Annual Essay Contest

Up to age 12
Write: Vegetarian Resource Group
P.O. Box 1463
Baltimore, MD 21203
E-mail: TheVRG@aol.com
Internet: http://www.vrg.org/
Call: Debra Wasserman, VRG Codirector
Main: 410-366-8343

Your passion for bacon cheeseburgers won't disqualify you from entering an essay on some aspect of vegetarianism. Perhaps the organizers of this contest hope that your research will lead you to join Madonna, Plato, Leonardo da Vinci, and Albert Einstein in not eating any meat, fish, or poultry. You might even become a vegan, which means using no dairy, wool, leather, eggs, silk, or any other animal products.

Write two to three pages on any aspect of vegetarianism. Postmark deadline is May 1. The prize is a $50 U.S. Savings Bond for each of three age divisions.

I strongly believe that it is wrong to kill animals, especially to eat them. I do not think they deserve to die like that. What did they do to us which allows us to harm them? In my opinion, it is extremely cruel and wrong to kill our marvelous animals, which are already becoming extinct. . . .

. . . if people are so worried about getting fat, why don't they stop stuffing themselves full of animal fat and eat fruits and vegetables instead? They are energizing and usually fat-free! I participate in many sports, such as wrestling and soccer, and can still maintain the energy and enthusiasm required.

Excerpt from "A Concern for Animals and the Environment" by 1997 cowinner Darren Legge, 11, Englewood, Colorado. Courtesy of the Vegetarian Resource Group.

🍎 Writing! Contests

Grade 6
Write: General Learning Communications
900 Skokie Boulevard, Suite 200
Northbrook, IL 60062-4028
Call: Alan Lenhoff, Editor
Main: 847-205-3000
Fax: 847-564-8197

Writing! magazine sponsors an annual contest for fiction and nonfiction. The theme changes each year. "Mystery" was the 1996–97 theme. Details are published in the first issue of the school year. (This magazine is sold in bulk for use in classrooms. See chapter 4.)

Entries should be 650 to 1,000 words long. Postmark deadline is early January. Prizes are $150, $100, and $50 for each of the two categories and two grade divisions.

The Writing Conference Contests

Grades K–6
Write: The Writing Conference

Attn: Dr. John H. Bushman, Director
P.O. Box 664
Ottawa, KS 66067
E-mail: witeconf@idir.net
Internet: http://scrtec.rtec.org/writing

Guidelines for the year's contests become available September 1. You can request them by E-mail as well as regular mail.

Writers of the best three essays win a plaque. Winning entries are published in *The Writers' Slate* (see chapter 4). First-place winners are invited to attend the Conference on Writing and Literature in Lawrence, Kansas, each spring.

Z-Team Contest

Ages 10–12
Write: Zillions
Consumers Union
101 Truman Avenue
Yonkers, NY 10703-1057

Readers of *Zillions*, the kids' magazine from the publishers of *Consumer Reports*, get a chance each year to become members of the "Z-Team." Each team member gets a T-shirt and gets to help review products like handheld video games for future issues of *Zillions*.

To win one of the 100 slots on the team, you must write a brief essay on the year's topic. One year you had to write about the funniest thing that happened to you in school that year in seventy-five or fewer words. Another year you had to imagine your first day on the job as the youngest-ever editor of *Zillions*. You were allowed to write 100 words in between the opening line of "My mind was buzzing with brilliant ideas, when BLAM!" and the final line of " 'You're a genius!' they exclaimed."

See the announcement in the March/April issue. The deadline is June 1.

See also:
AMERICAN HISTORY ESSAY CONTEST (chapter 6, under section "History")
HOMETOWN TREES KIDS ART CONTEST (chapter 6, under section "Multidiscipline Competitions")
LITTLE GREEN CREATIVE ARTS PROJECT (chapter 1, under section "Art")
NATIONAL HISTORY DAY COMPETITION (chapter 6, under section "History")
PROJECT ENVIRONMENT ESSAY AND POSTER CONTEST (chapter 1, under section "Art")
REFLECTIONS PROGRAM (chapter 1, under section "Art")
YOUTH HONOR AWARDS (chapter 3, under section "Fiction")
YOUTH WRITING CONTEST (this chapter, under section "Journalism")

Journalism

Disney Adventures Junior Reporter Contest

Ages 7–12
Write: **Disney Adventures**
114 Fifth Avenue
New York, NY 10011-5690
E-mail: DAKidStuff@aol.com
Direct: 212-807-5818
Fax: 212-807-5499

Each year *Disney Adventures* looks for twenty-five kid reporters to keep this magazine on the cutting edge of cool. To help with your assignments, you'll be given a *D.A.* press kit that includes a camera and tape recorder.

Each year the magazine comes up with a different contest to select its student news team. Once it asked would-be reporters to create a newsletter of 300 to 600 words that contained three articles, including a made-up celebrity interview. Another time they had to poll ten of their friends about "the ultimate summer vacation."

Write for the official entry blank and rules, or see the January issue of *Disney Adventures*. Submit your entry from mid-December to mid-January.

Earth & Sky Young Producers Contest

Grades K–6
Write: **Earth & Sky** *Radio Series*
P.O. Box 2203
Austin, TX 78768
Internet: http://www.earthsky.com/
E-mail: people@earthsky.com
Main: 512-477-4441
Fax: 512-477-4474

Open to students the world over, this contest lets you play producer of the popular radio show *Earth & Sky*. No doubt you've heard one of the brief daily broadcasts, since more than 950 stations carry them! Check the Web site to find out where and when to tune in. If you are too far from a station that carries the show, you can hear the broadcasts by connecting to the show's Web site. You can also read the scripts.

You and (if you want) one teammate will write a ninety-second script in English on a science or nature topic, then record it. Write (no SASE needed!) or send E-mail to request several pages of guidelines that cover things like what makes a good script, how to get a high-quality recording, how not to violate anyone's copyright, and more. Inquire anytime.

Entry deadline is December 1. Grand prize is a $1,000 U.S. Savings Bond. Four finalist teams win $500 bonds. All five winning entries are played on the air by *Earth & Sky* during May. All participants receive a certificate stating that they are a "Young Producer for *Earth & Sky*."

Kay Snow Writing Awards

All ages
Write: Willamette Writers
9045 SW Barbur Boulevard, Suite 5A
Portland, OR 97219
E-mail: wilwrite@teleport.com
Main: 503-452-1592
Fax: 503-452-0372

The Willamette Writers named this nationwide contest in honor of the founder of their organization, which serves published and aspiring writers. Entries from students (ages eighteen and under) are judged separately from adult entries. One year a six-year-old won the student division in the poetry category.

The word *adult* in a category name refers to the intended reader; the writer can be anyone, including a kid. Categories include nonfiction article for an adult market, adult short story, and juvenile short story or article. Write up to 1,500 words. There is also a category for scripts, partial or complete, of the same length. Poetry is the final category. Enter one to three poems, single-spaced, with a maximum length of five pages for the total entry.

The entry fee for nonmembers is $15 per entry per category entered. Enter from January until May 15. Prizes are $200, $100, and $50 in all categories. Awards are given at the WW annual banquet in August.

NewsCurrents Student Editorial Cartoon Contest

Grades K-6
Write: Editor
NewsCurrents
P.O. Box 52
Madison, WI 53701-0052

Internet: http://www.ku.com/carcontest.html
Call: Matt Cibula, Marketing Guy
Main: 800-356-2303
Fax: 608-831-1570

Submit as many cartoons as you wish. Each year's best 100 are published by Zino Press Children's Books in a book called *Editorial Cartoons by Kids.*

On the back of your cartoon print your name, grade, school, school
address, school phone number, and your teacher's name. Deadline is
March 1. Prizes for each grade division are U.S. Savings Bonds of
$100, $75, and $50.

Scholastic Press Freedom Award

All ages
Write: Student Press Law Center
1101 Wilson Boulevard, Suite 1910
Arlington, VA 22209
E-mail: splc@capaccess.org
Internet: http://splc.org/
Call: Mark Goodman, Executive Director
Main: 703-807-1904

Although this award has never been won by any student in a grade
lower than ninth grade, Mark Goodman says that could change,
owing to the rise of student-created, Internet-based news organizations.

Any individual student, student newspaper, magazine, yearbook,
or broadcast station may be nominated. Nominees should have demonstrated a responsible use of press freedom through writing and ac-
tions, such as the ability to raise difficult but important issues in news
coverage and report on them responsibly, representing all sides of the
issue equally. Nominations should clearly explain why the nominee
deserves the SPFA and should include examples of the nominee's
work.

Annual deadline for nominations is August 1. The award is presented in November at the national convention of the National Scholastic Press Association/Journalism Education Association.

One winner was Stacey Burns, former editor in chief of the *Hawkeye,* at Mountlake Terrace High School in Mountlake Terrace, Washington. She refused to give police copies of unpublished photos taken by the newspaper of a 1995 fight between Asian-American and white students in the school parking lot. Burns argued that students wouldn't trust the newspaper or give it interviews if it acted as an investigative arm of the police department.

Youth Writing Contest

Grade 6
Write: Outdoor Writers Association of America
2017 Cato Avenue, Suite 101
State College, PA 16801-2768
E-mail: 76711.1725@compuserve.com
Internet: http://www.ono.com/org/owaa/owaa.html
Call: Eileen King, Executive Assistant
Main: 814-234-1011

Your poem or prose on an "outdoor" topic must have been published somewhere to qualify for this contest. Publication in your student newspaper, club newsletter, or school literary collection counts just as much as being published in *National Geographic,* so that hurdle isn't much more than knee-high.

The sole criterion for judging is "excellent writing," so it's how you write and not what you've done that matters. A cleverly written story about bird-watching from your backyard hammock would do better than a poorly written account of climbing a mountain.

Submit one original tear sheet—that is, the actual newspaper or magazine page on which your writing appeared. The publication name and date must be visible on the tear sheet. Enter by the end of January.

Winners are announced at the OWAA annual conference in June. Junior division (grades 6–8) prizes are $100, $75, and $50.

Speech

🍎 Civic Oration Contest

Grades 5–6

Write: Modern Woodmen of America *(See page 21 for contact and other information about the contest.)*

Grab that microphone and talk! This contest may be held in any school in the continental United States by arrangement with an area representative of the MWA, a fraternal insurance company. If you can't find an MWA representative locally, contact the home office (listed above) to be matched with one.

Over 85,000 students a year enter this contest. Each participant speaks for three to five minutes on the current year's topic. "An American Invention" was the topic in 1997. A minimum of twelve students per school must participate.

Schools hold their contest anytime between January and May. There are trophies and certificates for school-level competitions. Winners advance through district and regional contests to the national competition in July. First prize is a $1,000 "savings plan" paid to the winner when he or she reaches "legal age."

Optimist International Contests

Write: Optimist International
Programs Department
4494 Lindell Boulevard
St. Louis, MO 63108
Internet: http://www.optimist.org/
Call: Helen Sykes, Project Coordinator
Main: 314-371-6000
Fax: 314-371-6006

These contests are open to residents of the United States, Canada, and Jamaica. You'll need to enter via your local Optimist Club, but that should be no problem. There are 4,000 clubs with 150,000 members. But if you can't find one near you, check with your chamber of commerce. The 1997 topic was "My Vision of Tomorrow's World."

1. OPTIMIST INTERNATIONAL COMMUNICATION CONTEST FOR THE DEAF AND HARD OF HEARING

Grades K–6

Participants must be recognized by the educational system as hearing impaired and must be educated as such. Students make a four- to five-minute presentation on the annual theme. District winners receive $1,500 scholarships. The competition date varies by district.

2. OPTIMIST INTERNATIONAL ORATORICAL CONTEST

Up to age 12

Actors Julia Roberts and Neil Patrick Harris are past winners of this contest, along with politicians and businesspeople from across the United States and Canada. Beginning each October, more than 10,000 schools join with local Optimist Clubs to stage this contest. Some 30,000 students speak for four to five minutes in hopes of winning scholarships worth a total of $150,000. Canadians may speak French.

3

Get Creative

Fiction and Poetry

Once upon a time, a student entered a story in a contest. It won first place. The student wrote more stories, each better than the last. That led to talk show appearances, sales of film rights, and breakfast cereal endorsements. One story inspired a menu item at Planet Hollywood.

The student had a friend who entered and won poetry contests. A rock band set the poems to music and toured sixty cities on five continents. Their CD went triple platinum in eleven days. NASA bought a copy to send into space in case the Voyager program is ever revived. A newly independent country adopted one poem as its national anthem.

"Can you handle the fame and pressure?" the media demanded. "Oh, sure," the two students replied. They continued to enter contests, maybe even the ones listed here! And they lived happily ever after.

Only a fairy tale? Yes—until you make it come true.

By the way, many poetry contests are sponsored by state poetry societies. Usually you can enter even if you live elsewhere; check the rules.

Fiction

Adlyn M. Keffer Memorial Short Story Writing Contest

Grades 4–6
Write: National Story League
c/o Dr. Richard Shepherd
984 Roelofs Road
Yardley, PA 19067
Call: Dr. Richard Shepherd, Chair
Main: 215-493-5256

Enter from January 1 to March 31. Your story must be "suitable for telling," original, and under 2,000 words. League members enter free; others pay $5.

Top prize is $20. The league's magazine, *Story Art,* has for one year the first right (but not the obligation) to print the winning stories.

American Girl Short Story Contest

Write: American Girl
Short Story Contest
8400 Fairway Place
Middleton, WI 53562-0986
E-mail: ageditor@ag.pleasantco.com
Internet: http://www.pleasantco.com/
Call: Magazine Dept. Assistant
Main: 608-836-4848
Fax: 608-831-7089

American Girl magazine targets eight- to twelve-year-olds, but counts many teens among its readers. Girls of any age may enter the short story contest.

And what makes this contest fun to enter year after year? The rules: They're never the same twice. Once contestants were assigned a theme. Another time, they had to begin their stories with a given sentence. Still another time, they were given a sentence but could use it anywhere in their story. For the latest twist, check the contest announcement in the November/December issue.

Here's what doesn't change: Limit your story to eight handwritten or three typed pages. Don't write about American Girls Collection characters (dolls in historical period dress, sold by an affiliated company). A parent must sign your entry. Winning stories are published in the July/August issue.

> *Evany Mayer searched her pockets for a very important piece of paper. Today Mr. Nicholas had given everyone in her class the name and address of an out-of-state pen pal, with instructions to correspond for at least six weeks over the summer and then write a summary of their pen-pal experience.*
>
> *Evany finally found the wad. "Lindsey Camarro, 1-L Royal Oaks Apartments, Sparrow Creek, Pennsylvania," she read out loud. She pulled out some of her favorite stationery and began talking to the blank paper. "Why would someone want to hear about my boring life? Lindsey doesn't know anything about me, so I'll just tell her what I wish my life was like!" Evany began to write. She put some truths into her letter, but as she wrote it became an adventure in pretending.*
>
> Excerpt from "Pen Pal Problems" by 1997 cowinner Shannon Krizni, 13, New Jersey. *American Girl* vol. 5, no. 4 © copyright 1997 by Pleasant Company. Reprinted by permission of Pleasant Company.

Children's Creative Writing Campaign

Up to age 12
Write: Creative Director
P.O. Box 999

Cooper Station
New York, NY 10276
Direct: 212-228-3041
Fax: 212-228-6574

Everyone should enter this "contest," because everyone wins! The purpose of the Children's Creative Writing Campaign is to encourage children to enjoy the process of writing. Some entries are poems as short as four lines. Two in 1996 were novels written by eleven-year-old girls! Other unusual entries were radio plays, interactive games, and comics.

The campaign relies mostly on teachers to involve their students. But you kids (particularly home schoolers) may take action on your own. Contact CCWC in the fall to obtain current information. You will need to attach an official form when submitting your writing.

Although CCWC suggests catagories of writing for those who want them, you are free to write about anything you wish. Make sure you are original, though. No takeoffs of TV shows, movies, or books allowed. Be imaginative! And write clearly.

The entries are sorted by age group and sent to readers who are professional screenwriters, animators, and children's authors. If a reader thinks that a piece of writing stands out among those by similar-aged students, then the writer qualifies as a semifinalist. If two readers think so, then the writer is a finalist, the highest ranking.

Virtually all participants receive an award certificate. Special-ed kids and students as young as five have been finalists. There is no limit on the number of participants, semifinalists, or finalists.

Finalists receive, in addition to a certificate, a $100 U.S. Savings Bond. Their schools get a $100 contribution to the library. In 1996 Microsoft donated its "Creativity" software to finalists and their schools.

CyberKids/CyberTeens International Writing and Art Contest

Ages 7–12
Write: Mountain Lake Software (*See page 8 for contact and other information about the contest.*)

Write a short story of up to fifteen pages. Stories may be written by more than one person, but whoever is listed first will receive the prize and be responsible for sharing it with his or her cocreators. Deadline for receipt of entries is the end of the year. You can submit your story by E-mail or regular mail. Voting runs through the middle of March. Prizes have included an Apple Power Macintosh, WACOM graphics tablets, cash, software, and books.

> *Not every mother cat goes through the problems I did. Do you want to hear about it? OK, here we go!*
>
> *Well, it all started in Amarillo, Texas, in the middle of winter when my kittens and I lived in an old abandoned shack near Cat Claw Alley. My problem occurred when my smallest daughter, Samantha, was learning her name. Her name had three syllables or meows in it. She pronounced her name correctly the first time; then she did something wrong. It sounded like this—meow, meow, bark!*
>
> Excerpt from "Cats Can't Bark" by 1995 cowinner Addie May, 10, San Carlos, California. Courtesy of the author.

Disney Adventures Story Contests

Ages 7–12
Write: Disney Adventures
114 Fifth Avenue
New York, NY 10011-5690
Call: Michelle Ernst
Main: 212-633-4400
Direct: 212-807-5818
Fax: 212-807-5499

Disney Adventures magazine has two story-writing contests. You'll need the official entry forms. Get them from the magazine or write to the above address.

If you love mysteries, create one in the Mystery Story Contest. Create a detective character and leave some clues for him or her as well as readers to find in your story of up to 1,000 words. Send it in by early April. Grand prize is publication and a set of Casebusters books autographed by author Joan Lowery Nixon.

There's also the Scary Stories Contest. Postmark deadline falls in June for your bloodcurdling tale of up to 1,000 words. A celebrity judge picks the winners. Grand prize is publication, plus enough scary books to fill a mummy's tomb.

Lines in the Sand Short Fiction Contest

All ages
Write: LeSand Publications
1252 Terra Nova Boulevard
Pacifica, CA 94044
Call: Barbara Less, Associate Editor
Main: 415-355-9069

Recently a high school junior beat an English teacher and other writers in this magazine's previous short story contest. "We were really shocked," Associate Editor Barbara Less says. But that wasn't the only surprise. Another high school junior earned an honorable mention. "If the story grabs us, and is good, anybody has a chance," Less says. So what are you waiting for?

Submit up to 2,000 words. Write any kind of story you want, but use "good taste" since *Lines in the Sand* magazine's readers are as young as seven. Enter your story with a $5 fee by October 31. Winners are printed in the January/February awards issue. First Place wins $50.

Paul A. Witty Outstanding Literature Award

Grades K–6
Write: International Reading Association (See page 54 for contact and other information about the contest.)

You may submit up to five poems or a single work of prose (short story, essay, or even a play) of around 1,000 words.

Postmark deadline is always February 1. Winners will be determined by mid-March, with the awards of at least $25 made at the IRA annual convention in late April or early May.

Read Writing and Art Awards

Grade 6; U.S. citizens only
Write: Read Magazine (*See page 29 for contact and other information about the contest.*)

Remember the boy in the movie *Home Alone*? His family picked on him so much that he thought it would be nice if they all disappeared . . . until they really did! Talk about a character in conflict!

That kind of person should populate your fiction entry in this contest. The judges want believable characters engaged in a clear conflict. So keep them on the edge of their seats throughout your five- to six-page story (typed double-spaced). Write any kind of story: adventure, suspense, humor, drama, mystery, historical fiction, and so on. Advice from the judges: Revise, revise, revise, just as professional writers do.

Enter by mid-December. Top prize is $100 and inclusion in the May student issue of *Read*. The editors would love to get more submissions from sixth graders.

Scenario Writing

Grades 4–6; U.S. citizens only
Write: Future Problem Solving Program
318 West Ann Street
Ann Arbor, MI 48104-1337
E-mail: fpsolv@aol.com
Internet: http://www.fpsp.org/

Main: 313-998-7377
Direct: 313-998-7876
Fax: 313-998-7663

An FPSP scenario is a short short story not exceeding 1,500 words. Using characters and a plot, it predicts the future at least twenty years from now but is written as though that future were the present.

You will write one or two scenarios, depending on whether your school registers with FPSP for the year-long program ($50 per, student) or the competitive round ($25 per student).

Winning scenarios advance to state, regional, and then the international competition in June at the University of Michigan. Prizes include U.S. Savings Bonds, certificates, and trophies.

The World's Best Short Short Story Contest

All ages
Write: Contest Coordinator
World's Best Short Short Contest
English Department
Florida State University
Tallahassee, FL 32306-1036
Direct: 904-644-4230

Can you write a great story in just 250 words? If so, a check for $100 and a crate of Florida oranges awaits you. Submit one typed, double-spaced page and a $1 entry fee by mid-February. Anyone may enter.

The winning story is announced in mid-May. It also is published in the FSU English department's magazine, *Sun Dog: The Southeast Review,* and in a separate broadsheet. Finalists are also published in *Sun Dog.*

The Writing Conference Contests

Grades K–6
Write: The Writing Conference (See page 56 for contact and other information about the contest.)

Guidelines for the year's contests become available September 1. You can request them by E-mail as well as regular mail.

Writers of the best three short stories win a plaque. Winning entries are published in *The Writers' Slate* (see chapter 4). First-place winners are invited to attend the Conference on Writing and Literature in Lawrence, Kansas, each spring.

Youth Honor Awards

Ages 7–12
Write: Skipping Stones
Youth Honor Awards
P.O. Box 3939
Eugene, OR 97403-0939
Internet: http://www.nonviolence.org/~nvweb/skipping/
Contact: Arun Toke, Editor
Main: 541-342-4956

The Youth Honor Awards recognize creative writing, artistic abilities, and community service. Art should promote multicultural awareness, nature and ecology, social issues, peace, and nonviolence. Be as imaginative or realistic as you choose.

You can submit original artwork like drawings, cartoons, paintings, or photo essays with captions. Non-English and bilingual entries are welcome.

Write to *Skipping Stones* magazine to learn the annual theme. The 1998 theme is "Multicultural and Nature Awareness . . ." Annual postmark deadline is June 25. Enclose an SASE and $3 fee for each entry. Low-income entrants and subscribers get one free entry.

All entrants receive the autumn issue containing the top ten entries, which also win certificates, five multicultural and/or nature books, and a subscription to *Skipping Stones.*

(Scene: A company conference table in the year 2025)
Flora Green: *Our creation of Bird Sanctuary was entirely success-ful. Give Martin Purple a cheer for a job well done. (Cheers) And our construction of Wildlife Habitat Reserve is well under way. Ms. Down, as head of the bulldozing committee, give us an update of your progress.*
Tiria Down: *We are getting all the strip malls and concrete out of the way. It'll be done in no time!*

> Excerpt from "Modern Development" by Anaar Eastoak-Siletz, age 11, Santa Rosa, California. Courtesy of *Skipping Stones,* September/October 1996.

Zino Games

Zino Press Children's Books
P.O. Box 52
Madison, WI 53701
Internet: http://www.ku.com/zinogame1.html

Every few months this publisher holds a story-writing contest for kids. Stories must address the topic specified in the rules. In one contest, the rules called for the best story about a real or imaginary pig.

"We will pick one story that makes us laugh the hardest, cry the loudest, or think the deepest," the publisher says. Besides that, the story must be original, not "too gross to print in an average newspa-per," and not too long or short. "Use your best judgment," the pub-lisher says.

Submit by mail or by filling in the form on the Web site. Prizes are children's books.

See also:
BYLINE *STUDENT CONTESTS* (chapter 2, under section "Essay")

GRANDMOTHER EARTH NATIONAL WRITING CONTEST
(chapter 2, under section "Essay")

KAY SNOW WRITING AWARDS (this chapter, under section
"Poetry")

LITTLE GREEN CREATIVE ARTS PROJECT (chapter 1, under
section "Art")

NATIONAL WRITERS ASSOCIATION CONTESTS (this
chapter, under section "Poetry")

REFLECTIONS PROGRAM (chapter 1, under section "Art")

*WRITERS UNLIMITED ANNUAL INTERNATIONAL
LITERARY COMPETITION* (this chapter, under section
"Poetry")

WRITING! CONTESTS (chapter 2, under section "Essay")

YOUTH WRITING CONTEST (chapter 2, under section
"Journalism")

Poetry

Alabama State Poetry Society Contests

All ages
Write: Debbie Parvin
ASPS Contest Chairman
426 Woodhaven Court
Montgomery, AL 36117

Contests are held several times a year. The fall contest has seven categories open to everyone (including nonresidents and students). The entry fee is $2 per poem. Prizes range up to $50.

AMHAY Literary Contest

Up to age 12
*Write: American Morgan Horse Association (See page 1 for contact
and other information about the contest.)*

If writing poems about horses is your "mane" thing, this is your chance. The original Justin Morgan horse, described as having "tremendous endurance and a delicate head," was the only horse to sire a distinct breed in the United States.

Check with AMHA for the current year's theme and official entry blank. Past themes included "Olympic-Size Morgan Dreams" and "If My Morgan Could Talk." Your poem must be postmarked by the start of October. Top prize is $25.

Ann Arlys Bowler Poetry Prize

Grade 6; U.S. citizens only
Write: Read Magazine *(See page 29 for contact and other information about the contest.)*

Submit up to three poems, typed, any genre, none longer than one page. Include the entry coupon from *Read* magazine. Don't include a letter. Don't bother sending a stamped return envelope. *Read* can neither acknowledge receipt of your entry nor return it later. Do not enter by E-mail! Beat the mid-December deadline.

Then sit back and imagine your envious friends perusing your prizewinning poem in the May student issue of *Read*. Think about how you will spend your $100 prize (there are six winners). Bask in the glory of the congratulatory letter that top winners receive from the U.S. poet laureate.

And keep writing.

Arizona State Poetry Society Annual Contest

All ages
Write: Audrey Opitz
317 Hackney Avenue
Globe, AZ 85501

Entry fees are $1 or $2, depending on the category. Prizes range up to $50.

California Federation of Chaparral Poets Contests

All ages
Write: California Federation of Chaparral Poets
Attn: Pegasus Buchanan
Monthly Contest Editor
1422 Ashland Avenue
Claremont, CA 91711

Every month the federation sponsors a different contest. Postmark deadline is midnight of the last day of the contest month. Entry fee is $1. Prizes are $25, $15, and $10.

California State Poetry Society Contest

All ages
Write: California State Poetry Society
Attn: Ernestine Hoff Emrick
Contest Chair
2780 Hillcrest Drive
La Verne, CA 91750

This contest is open to "all poets in the United States." Enter an original, unpublished poem up to forty lines. It must be in English and not have won prize money previously. Entry should be postmarked between March 1 and May 31. Entry fee is $3 per poem. Prizes are $100, $70, and $30. Ten honorable mentions win $10 each. Winners are notified by July 15. Winning poems will be considered for publication in the society's publication, *CQ*.

Connecticut Poetry Society Contests

All ages
Write: Connecticut Poetry Society
41 Sunnybrook Bend
Waterbury, CT 06708

The society sponsors two contests a year. Entries in the Joesph E. Brodine Poetry Contest must be postmarked between May 1 and July 31. For the Wallace W. Winchell contest, the postmark deadline falls between October 1 and December 31.

Nonmembers pay $2 per poem to enter up to five poems of no more than forty lines each. Poems must be original, unpublished, and not a prizewinner elsewhere. Prizes are $150, $100, and $50, plus publication in *Connecticut River Review,* a national poetry journal.

Florida State Poets Association Annual Contest

All ages
Write: Flo Ruppert
P.O. Box 97
Roseland, FL 32957

Nonmembers pay $1 or $2 per poem, depending on which of the twenty-five categories is entered. Your poem must be original, unpublished, and not submitted for judging or publication elsewhere. It must not have won more than $10 in prior contests. Postmark deadline is August 15. Prizes range up to $150.

Illinois State Poetry Society Contests

All ages
Write: Glenna Holloway
Contest Chair
913 East Bailey Road
Naperville, IL 60565

Categories include free verse, formal verse, and sonnet. Prizes range up to $100. Your poem cannot have been published, but it may have been a winner elsewhere. Annual postmark deadline is August 15.

Indiana State Federation of Poetry Clubs Contests

All ages
Write: Indiana State Federation of Poetry Clubs
Attn: Dottie Mack
Contest Director
P.O. Box 643
Huntertown, IN 46748

Poets from Arizona, Illinois, Utah, and Washington won a recent ISFPC contest, so you definitely don't have to be from Indiana to win this one! All students can enter the adult categories, but only Indiana students can enter the student categories.

The federation holds three contests a year. The Fall Poets Rendezvous has twenty-five categories, including the two for students. Prizes range up to $50. Postmark deadline is September 1. Entry fee is a flat $5, for which you can enter as many categories as you want. You must submit a different poem for each.

The Poets Winter Forum contest has a *receipt* deadline of January 15. The Poets Summer Stanzas contest has a *receipt* deadline of June 15.

The Jabberwocky Poetry Contest

All ages
Write: Georgia State Poetry Society
Attn: Emery L. Campbell
Contests Chairman
369 Cottage Way
Lawrenceville, GA 30244

Remember the time you swore never to write poems that rhyme because you couldn't find a word that rhymed with *orange*? This contest is for you, because you get to make up words. "The wackier the better," the society says.

Your poem of up to thirty lines should introduce at least six new words to the English language. Include a glossary in case the judges don't understand them at first. Postmark deadline is the end of October. Entry fee is $1 for nonmembers. Prizes are $25, $15, and $10.

Kansas State Poetry Society Contests

All ages
Write: Kansas State Poetry Society
Attn: Sister Mary Faith
302 North Fifth Street
Atchison, KS 66002

There's no fee to enter KSPS fall and spring contests. Each has about fifteen categories: haiku, sonnet, and so on. Anyone may enter. Deadlines fall at the end of March and September. Submitted poems may be published in the KSPS magazine, *Sunflower Petals*. Past prizes have included certificates and pictures of George Washington.

Kay Snow Writing Awards

All ages
Write: **Willamette Writers** *(See page 60 for contact and other information about the contest.)*

The Willamette Writers named this nationwide contest in honor of the founder of their organization, which serves published and aspiring writers. Students (ages eighteen and under) and adults enter the same categories, but student entries are judged separately. One year a six-year-old won the student division in the poetry category.

Enter one to three poems, single-spaced, with a maximum length of five pages for the total entry.

The entry fee for nonmembers is $15 per entry per category entered. Enter from January until May 15. Prizes are $200, $100, and $50 in all categories. Awards are made at the WW annual banquet in August.

Kentucky State Poetry Society Annual Contest

All ages
Write: **Kentucky State Poetry Society**
Attn: **Miriam Woolfolk**
3289 Hunting Hills Drive
Lexington, KY 40515-4662
Call: **Miriam Woolfolk, Editor, Pegasus**
Direct: **606-271-4662**

This contest has more than forty separately judged categories. Would your verse fit under Poems Written After Midnight or One Shining Moment?

There are special categories reserved for sutdents. You are allowed to hand-print your poems if you can't type.

The overall contest is open to anyone, anywhere. Write for the rules in the fall. Entry deadline is the end of June. It costs nothing to enter the student categories, where the top prize is $15. Other categories cost $1 per poem, except Grand Prix. That has a $5 fee and a $100 top prize.

Winning poems are published in an issue of *Pegasus,* the publication of the Kentucky State Poetry Society. If you can't attend the annual awards banquet, KSPS will mail your award.

The League of Minnesota Poets

All ages
Write: Doris Stengel
Contest Chair
1510 South Seventh Street
Brainerd, MN 56401

Students pay no entry fee for the Students Award category. Otherwise, nonmembers pay $1 per category entered. There are seventeen categories with prizes up to $75.

Louisiana State Poetry Society Contest

All ages
Write: LSPS Contest Director
P.O. Box 77721
Baton Rouge, LA 70879

You can enter each of the nine open categories one time. Fee is $1 per poem. Deadline is early September. Prizes range up to $50.

Mississippi Poetry Society Contests

All ages
Write: Mississippi Poetry Society
Dr. Emory D. Jones, President
608 North Pearl Street
Iuka, MS 38852-2223

Students who pay the $3 membership fee enter all categories for free. If you do not pay, you can still enter the Student Award category for free. Prizes are $15, $10, and $5. Prizes in seventeen other categories range up to $100.

Mississippi Valley Poetry Contest

All ages
Write: North American Literary Escadrille
P.O. Box 3188
Rock Island, IL 61204-3188
E-mail: easywri571@aol.com
Call: Jim Arpy, Board Member
Direct: 309-762-3989

Enter from one to five poems on any topic from January till the end of March. Students may only enter the student division. Pay a $3 fee whether you enter one poem or five.

Elementary school poets can win prizes of $50. Prizes are awarded at a ceremony in Moline, Illinois. If you can't attend, you'll get your prize by mail.

National Council of State Garden Clubs Poetry Contest

Grades K–6
Write: Your state garden club

This is a popular contest: It isn't unusual for a single school to have 700 students want to enter poems. Unfortunately, schools may select only one poem per grade to send on to their state garden club for judging.

The theme changes each year. Once it was "America's Birds." Winning state entries advance to the national competition in December. There is no prize other than the honor of seeing the winning poems appear in an NCSGC publication.

National Poetry Day Contest

All ages
Write: National Poetry Day Contest
Attn: Jeanette C. Maes
Poetry Day Chairman
Massachusetts State Poetry Society
64 Harrison Avenue
Lynn, MA 01905

Choose among twenty-five categories, each with a different subject like "A Snowstorm," "Courage," or "Sisters." A $3 fee lets you enter as many categories as you like, but only once and with a different poem for each. Poems must not have won more than an honorable mention elsewhere, and must not have been published or submitted simultaneously to other contests.

Deadline for receipt of entries is August 1. Prizes range up to $30.

National Writers Association Contests

All ages
Write: National Writers Association
1450 South Havana
Aurora, CO 80012
E-mail: Sandywrter@aol.com
Internet: Sandy.NWA@GENIE.GEIS.COM
Call: Sandy Whelchel, Director
Main: 303-751-7844
Fax: 303-751-8593

The NWA has looked after the commercial interests of its 5,000 members since 1937. The following contests, open to all, aim to encourage the writing of poetry and fiction, and to recognize those who excel in the field. NWA uses only professional editors or agents as judges.

Awards are given at the NWA annual conference, always held in Colorado over the second weekend in June.

1. POETRY

An eight-year-old girl placed in this contest in 1996. "Kids write some of the best poetry we get," says an NWA executive. Enter from July 1. Postmark deadline is October 1. Size limit is forty lines. Enclose a $10 fee. Pay another $16 if you want NWA to critique your poem. Use the official entry blank or a photocopy. Prizes are $100, $50, $25, and $15. Authors retain all rights, but NWA requests anthology rights for the first- through third-place winners.

2. SHORT STORY

A sixteen-year-old girl placed in this contest in 1995. You can read her story and other past winners by ordering them from NWA. Unpublished stories up to 5,000 words long may be entered from April 1 to July 1. Entry fee is $15. Prizes are $200, $100, and $50. NWA requests anthology rights for the top three stories.

Nevada Poetry Society National Contest

All ages
Write: Nevada Poetry Society
Attn: Sam Wood
Contest Chairman
P.O. Box 7014
Reno, NV 89510

Postmark deadline is August 31 in the Silver State. Entry fee is $2 per poem. The categories are free verse, traditional or new form, Nevada residents only, and humor. You can enter only one category, but you can submit as many poems for that category as you wish.

Poems must be original, not currently submitted elsewhere, and unpublished. They must not have won more than $10 in a previous contest. Prizes range up to $100. Winning poems are read at the October meeting of the Nevada Poetry Society.

New Jersey Poetry Society Contests

Write: Ellen Kisthardt
Contest Chairperson
195 West Millstream Road
Cream Ridge, NJ 08514

Entry fee is $2 for the first poem, $1 for each additional. Prizes range up to $75.

North Carolina Poetry Society Contests

All ages
Write: Leon Hinton

4618 North NC 62
Burlington, NC 27217
E-mail: lchinton@netpath.net

Nonmembers may enter the adult categories for a fee of $3 per poem. Only North Carolina residents may enter the student categories. Deadline is early January. Prizes range up to $25.

Ohio Poetry Day Contests

All ages
Write: Amy Jo Zook
3520 State Route 56
Mechanicsburg, OH 43044

Why would Pearl B. Seagall's sons "honor" her by sponsoring the Best Bad Poem Contest category? Why must those entries use the words *Jell-O, numbers, wrestling, mold,* and *massage*—twice each? The rules don't say. Why not make your own speculations the subject of your poem?

If that category doesn't grab you, there are twenty-four others open to all, and eleven more for Ohio natives or residents. Pay an $8 fee to enter as many as you want. Prizes range up to $75.

Pennsylvania Poetry Society Contest

All ages
Write: Lillian Tweedy
Contest Chairman
Pennsylvania Poetry Society
2488 New Franklin Road
Chambersburg, PA 17201

Only Pennsylvania students may aim for the Student Pegasus Awards, which have no entry fee. Other poets may enter the annual contest, which has twelve categories open to nonmembers. The fee is $2 per poem for up to three poems entered in the Grand Prize Award category. Prizes in that category are $100, $50, and $25. The other eleven open categories have a fee of $1.50, with a limit of one poem submitted per category. They offer prizes of $25, $15, and $10.

No poem may be submitted in multiple categories or be under consideration for publication or contests elsewhere. Poems must not have already won an award or have been published elsewhere.

Postmark deadline is mid-January. Winning poems are published in the annual book *PPS Prize Poems*.

Poetry Society of New Hampshire National Contest

All ages
Write: J. Barbara Simpson
PSNH National Contest Chairperson
30 Williams Street
Nashua, NH 03060-4009

Enter as often as you wish. Entry fee is $2 for your first poem, $1 each thereafter. Poems may not have won more than $10 elsewhere, be simultaneously submitted in other contests, or have been published.

In 1996, PSNH had one contest without a theme with an August 15 deadline. A second contest with a November 15 deadline had the theme "Let Us Give Thanks." Write at year's end for the coming year's contest details.

Prizes are $50, $25, and $10, plus publication in the society's magazine, *TOUCHSTONE*.

Poetry Society of Texas Annual Contests

All ages
Write: Poetry Society of Texas
Attn: Laura Birkelbach
Annual Contest Committee
3005 Stanford Drive
Plano, TX 75075

This is more like a single contest with around 100 categories, 18 of which are open to nonmembers. The Therese Lindsey Award has the largest prize, $500. It costs $5 to enter and has a fifty-line limit.

The other contests have prizes ranging from $25 to $400. They cost $2 per poem to enter. You may enter each category once, with a different poem for each. Deadline for receipt is September 15.

Poetry Society of Virginia Contests

All ages
Write: Claudia Gary Annis
217 Nottoway Street SE
Leesburg, VA 22075

Students enter one poem per category. (There is a separate category for sonnets.) The Middle School Prize has a limit of twenty-four lines and prizes of $25, $15, and $10.

Your poem must be original, in English, unpublished, not submitted for publication, and not entered in other contests. Submit two copies. Deadline is January 19 (Edgar Allan Poe's birthday).

Winners are announced at an awards luncheon in March.

Poets Roundtable of Arkansas Annual Poetry Day Awards

All ages
Write: Peggy Vining
Poets Roundtable of Arkansas
6817 Gingerbread Lane
Little Rock, AR 72204

One $5 fee lets you enter all twenty-seven categories. Postmark deadline is early September. Prizes range up to $1,000.

The Robert Penn Warren Poetry Awards

All ages
Write: Dr. Frank Anthony
New England Writers Contest
151 Main Street
P.O. Box 483
Windsor, VT 05089-0483

Postmark deadline is June 15 for this free verse contest. You pay $5 for each three poems you enter. Don't submit the same poems elsewhere at the same time. Prizes are $200, $100, and $50. The best thirty-three poems get published in *The Anthology of New England Writers*, an annual journal.

South Dakota State Poetry Society Contest

All ages
Write: SDSPS Contest

Attn: Myra Osterberg
P.O. Box 613
Salem, SD 57058-0613

Enter one poem per category, and don't enter the same poem in more than one category. Your poem must be unpublished and have won no more than $10 elsewhere. A single entry fee of $6 allows nonmembers to enter all categories except for the grand prize. In that category you may submit as many poems as you wish for a fee of $2 per poem.

Deadline is August 31. The grand-prize winner receives $75. Prizes in other categories are $25, $15, and $10.

Utah State Poetry Society Contest

All ages
Write: USPS
Attn: Elaine Ipson
449 Country Club
Stansburg Park, UT 84074

There are fifteen categories, all open to nonmembers. Entry fee is $2 per poem for nonmembers except in the Youth Contest category, which has no fee. Prizes range up to $50.

Send an SASE in the fall for the current year's rules. Postmark deadline on contest entries is the start of February.

West Virginia Poetry Society Annual Contest

All ages
Write: Melba Dungey
Contest Chairman

101 Jones Avenue
Morgantown, WV 26505

Only West Virginians can enter the three no-fee student categories, which range from kindergarten to twelfth grade. Students elsewhere can compete in the twenty-seven open categories. Nonmembers pay $1 per poem up to a maximum of $12.

Deadline is July 15. Prizes range up to $75. WVPS publishes the top three poems per category in its annual anthology.

Writers Unlimited Annual International Literary Competition

All ages
Write: Writers Unlimited
Attn: Nina Mason
910 Grant Avenue
Pascagoula, MS 39567-7222
Call: Nina Mason
Direct: 601-762-4230

A contest in which you write a single sentence? That's just one of the fifteen categories—many of which accept prose and poetry—in this literary competition.

Junior high and high school students may enter short story categories created just for them without paying a fee. The other categories are open to all. Enter as many as you want once each for a blanket $5 fee, except for Category I (narrative poem). That one has its own $2 fee.

Entry deadline is September 1. Prizes range up to $50.

See also:
BYLINE *STUDENT CONTESTS* (chapter 2, under section "Essay")

CHILDREN'S CREATIVE WRITING CAMPAIGN (this chapter, under section "Fiction")

GRANDMOTHER EARTH NATIONAL WRITING CONTEST (chapter 2, under section "Essay")

LITTLE GREEN CREATIVE ARTS PROJECT (chapter 1, under section "Art")

PAUL A. WITTY OUTSTANDING LITERATURE AWARD (this chapter, under section "Fiction")

REFLECTIONS PROGRAM (chapter 1, under section "Art")

YOUTH HONOR AWARDS (this chapter, under section "Fiction")

YOUTH WRITING CONTEST (chapter 2, under section "Journalism")

4

Send It In!

Opportunities to Publish Your Art,

Writing, and Photos

Artists, photographers, and writers alike should read this chapter. Your goal here is not to collect a prize, but to win acceptance of your work for publication. Magazine editors know that students create many stories and pictures that deserve to be seen and enjoyed by others. Since they get lots of submissions, though, editors are very picky. You have a right to be proud when an editor publishes your work, even if you receive no payment.

Usually you can submit work to magazines whether or not you subscribe. But you should read or at least be familiar with a magazine before submitting your writing or art. You'll have a better idea of what a magazine wants if you have seen other student work that it has published. If the magazine is not in your school or local library, write to the editor to ask for a sample copy. Sometimes samples are free, but not always.

Two kinds of publications are listed here. One kind focuses on creativity. These magazines exist primarily to publish what readers submit. Such publications are marked with an asterisk (*) before the name. The other kind focuses on special interests. They use some material supplied by readers, but mostly rely on professional writers and artists.

With special interest magazines, your best chance of getting published is to send in material that relates to the publication's overall interest or to the theme of a recent issue. If you can stick to that, your chances of being published with a special interest magazine might actually be better than with publications that rely on reader submissions.

*The Acorn

Grades K–6
Write: 1530 Seventh Street
Rock Island, IL 61201

This publication seeks poetry up to thirty-five lines and fiction up to 500 words. *The Acorn* doesn't accept writing about killing humans or animals. The editor especially looks for essays of up to 500 words on hopeful topics.

If the staff likes your writing, they will publish it—there is no payment. The July 1996 issue was five pages of typing paper, printed on a black-and-white photocopier and stapled. The subscription price is $10 for four issues. A sample issue costs $2.

*Authorship

All ages
Write: National Writers Association
1450 South Havana
Aurora, CO 80012
E-mail: Sandywrter@aol.com
Internet: Sandy.NWA@GENIE.GEIS.COM
Call: Sandy Whelchel, Director
Main: 303-751-7844
Fax: 303-751-8593

Authorship is published by the National Writers Association, which has looked after the commercial interests of its 5,000 members since 1937. The editors publish articles submitted by writers of all ages. "We take everything," says one of the executives there. (For NWA contests, see chapter 3, section "Poetry," under "National Writers Association Contests.")

Send an SASE for submission requirements. A subscription costs $18 for six issues a year.

*The Benton Courier

All ages
Write: Don Crowson
131 South First Street
Benton, AR 72015
E-mail: dcrowson@tce.net

Poets near and far submit their work to the weekly poetry column in this Arkansas newspaper. Enclose an SASE with your poem of sixteen or fewer lines, and if the newspaper uses it, you'll get back a clipping of your published poem.

Boomerang!

Ages 6–12
Write: Box 261c
La Honda, CA 94020
Toll free: 800-333-7858

Have you ever listened to a magazine? *Boomerang!* is a seventy-minute audiomagazine for kids that comes on cassette tape ($43.95 for twelve issues per year; $5 for a sample). It contains current events, history, and geography features, mysteries, letters to the editor, jokes, humorous commentary, phony commercials, interviews, tips on helping the environment, and more.

Kids can write letters to the producers and participate in the opinion polls that *Boomerang!* conducts. The producers also want kids to pitch ideas for features that the kids would create and record for inclusion in future issues, so start brainstorming.

*Children's Better Health Institute

Write: P.O. Box 567
Indianapolis, IN 46206
Main: 317-636-8881

CBHI publishes magazines that offer fun features for kids as well as advice on staying safe, fit, and healthy. The editors accept submissions from subscribers only in the form of letters, short stories, jokes and riddles, art, and poems. They also like a parent or teacher to verify that the material really was created by the student who submitted it. The magazines publish only work from students in the age groups that they target (see below). There is no payment or free copy. The magazines own all rights to published material.

Each magazine publishes eight issues a year. Issues are thirty-six or more pages, with color on most or all pages. Subscriptions are $16.95, except for *U*S*Kids*, a *Weekly Reader* magazine, which is $21.95. Call 800-829-5579 to subscribe.

1. CHILD LIFE

Ages 9–11
Write: Lise Hoffman, Editor

An Alien Under My Bed

I have an alien under my bed.
(I don't know how he got there.)
Some kids are lucky; they have monsters.

My dad says there's no such thing as aliens.
But I think he's wrong.
I see some really shiny eyes.
He has a red ray gun.
Instead of shooting lasers, I bet it's chewed up gum!
He's there only when all the lights are off.
(I wonder how he hides.)
He might hide in the corner of my bed.
He should get a prize.
He likes dark places.
(Why shouldn't I know! He's mine.)
But still he's free, trying to get me.
There's an alien under my bed!

By Scott Kersey, grade 3, Independence, Oregon.
Copyright © *Child Life*, April/May 1997.
Reprinted with permission.

2. CHILDREN'S DIGEST

"Preteen"
Write: Editor

3. CHILDREN'S PLAYMATE *MAGAZINE*

Ages 6–8
Write: Terry Harshmann, Editor

4. JACK AND JILL

Ages 7–10
Write: Daniel Lee, Editor

5. U*S*KIDS, *A* WEEKLY READER *MAGAZINE*

Ages 5–10
Write: Jeff Ayers, Editor

Rabbit

There was a very big hole,
Bigger than a mole.
In it lived a rabbit,
Who had a bad habit.
For he had a loud snore,
As loud as a lion's roar.
His friends hated that,
For it made a noisy habitat.

By Meet Doshi, age 8, Budd Lake, New Jersey.
Copyright © *U*S*Kids,* a *Weekly Reader*
magazine, March 1997. Reprinted with
permission.

Children's Surprises

Ages 5–12
Write: The Publishing Group, Inc.
1200 North Seventh Street
Minneapolis, MN 55411-4000
Internet: http://www.surprises.com/
Call: Tim Drake, Editor
Main: 612-522-1200, ext. 218
Fax: 612-522-1182

Every page of *Surprises* (as the magazine is better known) has an activity for kids: mazes, word scrambles, puzzles, and more. There is a "gallery" for artwork and poetry sent in by readers. And many issues feature story-writing contests. The thirty-two-page magazine has color throughout. It costs $15.95 for six issues a year.

Children's Television Workshop

Ages 6–12
Write: One Lincoln Plaza
New York, NY 10023

1. 3-2-1 CONTACT

E-mail: email321@aol.com

Did you have a real-life adventure? Write it down in 500 words or fewer. Include your name, age, address, and telephone number. Send it to *3-2-1 Contact*. If the editors print it, they will pay you $100. One girl wrote about being knocked overboard when her dad's fishing boat ran into a whale! This magazine has forty pages with color throughout. It costs $19.90 for ten issues a year.

2. KID CITY

Reader submissions of art and writing appear on the Kids Rule! pages in this magazine. There are also occasional writing contests. *Kid City* publishes ten issues a year. A subscription costs $19.70. The forty-page magazine has color on all pages.

Cobblestone Publishing

Ages 8–12
Write: 7 School Street
Peterborough, NH 03458
Internet: http://www.cobblestonepub.com/
Toll free: 800-821-0115
Main: 603-924-7209
Fax: 603-924-7380

The magazines published by Cobblestone take kids on voyages of discovery back in time, across cultural divides, or out to the frontiers of scientific knowledge.

1. CALLIOPE: WORLD HISTORY FOR YOUNG PEOPLE

Ages 8–12
Call: Rosalie Baker, Editor

Calliope welcomes reader contributions of letters, poems, and artwork. It also runs a different contest for readers each year. The magazine has a glossy color cover and fifty black-and-white pages. Each issue is organized around a world history topic, such as "The Doges of Venice" in the March/April 1997 issue. The subscription price is $18.95 for five issues a year.

2. COBBLESTONE: THE HISTORY MAGAZINE FOR YOUNG PEOPLE

Ages 8–12
Call: Meg Chorlian, Editor

Reader letters are sought regularly for *Cobblestone,* which focuses on American history. The magazine also features occasional contests tied to the issue's theme. Cobblestone's forty-eight pages are filled with lively articles, fun activities, and color and black-and-white images and illustrations. The subscription price is $24.95 for nine issues a year.

3. FACES: THE MAGAZINE ABOUT PEOPLE

Ages 8–12
Call: Carolyn Yoder, Editor

Reader submissions of letters, poems, and art are welcomed by *Faces,* a magazine devoted to world cultures. In an issue about Ireland, a contest asked readers to create an "illuminated manuscript," or a highly illustrated text, like the Book of Kells, a medieval Irish version of the Gospels known for its marvelous illustrations. *Faces* is a professionally produced magazine with a glossy color cover and forty black-

and-white pages. The subscription price is $23.95 for nine issues a year.

4. ODYSSEY: SCIENCE THAT'S OUT OF THIS WORLD

Ages 8–12
Call: Beth Armstrong, Editor

Odyssey explores science topics of current interest in a lively way. Letters are welcome, as are reader contributions for the "Future Forum" and "Ask Uly" features. The full-color magazine has about fifty pages. The subscription price is $24.95 for nine issues a year.

*Creative Kids

Ages 8–12
Write: Submissions Editor
Creative Kids
P.O. Box 8813
Waco, TX 76714-8813
E-mail: creative_kids@prufrock.com
Internet: http://www.prufrock.com/
Call: Libby Lindsey, Editor
Toll free: 800-998-2208
Main: 817-756-3337, ext. 312
Fax: 800-240-0333

The editors want cartoons, songs, stories between 800 and 900 words, puzzles, photographs, artwork, games and other activities, editorials, poetry, and plays by kids. Each issue also announces writing or art contests. Payment for publication is a copy of that issue. The magazine has a glossy color cover and about thirty pages inside with two colors. A subscription is $19.95 for four issues a year. Send an SASE for submission guidelines.

Mom and Dad had a meeting at 9 A.M. They left me alone for the whole morning. I couldn't have any friends over, and I was alone! This was going to be one boring morning. Then I remembered my closet.

I have a closet in my house that's long and narrow, and it seems to go on forever. I've never seen the back of it, so today, I decided to look.

I darted upstairs and went through the library to the back wall. I opened the closet door and pushed through the suits and came to a wall!?! What a disappointment. I kicked the wall out of frustration, and all of a sudden it swiveled around. I pushed it once and walked through. I found I was no longer walking on a hard, cold floor, but on soft, green grass.

Excerpt from "The Memory Chest" by Liana Gorman, age 10, Manchester, Connecticut. Courtesy of *Creative Kids.*

*Creative With Words Publications

Up to age 12
Write: P.O. Box 223226
Carmel, CA 93922
Call: Brigitta Geltrich, Editor
Fax: 408-655-8627

CWWP publishes about twelve anthologies a year, each devoted to a theme. *We Are Writers, Too!* is CWWP's annual anthology of student-only writing. Poems of up to twenty lines and prose up to 1,200 words are wanted. No violent, religious, or morally instructive material is accepted. Payment for publication is a discount of 20 percent on purchases of up to ten copies. Orders of ten copies or more receive a 30 percent discount. The regular price is $9 to $12 per copy.

Cricket

Up to age 12
Write: Cricket League
P.O. Box 300
Peru, IL 61354

Cricket publishes letters and brief book reviews by students. It has a new story, art, poetry, or photography contest each month. Entries must be on the specific theme given and follow the rules listed on the Cricket League page of each magazine. Include an SASE when corresponding.

The magazine is sixty-four pages, professionally published, with color throughout. A subscription costs $32.97 for 12 issues a year.

> *"Anna, hurry! We're going to miss our train!"*
> *"This stupid skirt keeps getting caught, Nora."*
> *The year was 1880, and Anna O'Brian and I, both fifteen, were running as fast as we could in our long, fussy skirts to catch the train for college in Minneapolis.*
> *Soon I realized that Anna was no longer following me. Then I heard her say, "Don't wait for me! I'll take the next train. Go now, run!"*
> *She'll make the next train, I thought. But I never saw Anna in college.*

Excerpt from "Telling the Past" by Carey Olson, age 11, Ellensburg, Washington, Courtesy of Cricket, May 1995.

Dolphin Log

Ages 7–12
Write: 777 United Nations Plaza, Fifth Floor
New York, NY 10017-3585
E-mail: cousteauny@aol.com

Internet: http://cousteau.edi.fr/cousteau
Call: Lisa Rao, Editor
Main: 212-949-6290
Fax: 212-949-6292

You would expect a publication of the Cousteau Society to feature fascinating underwater photos. After all, it was Jacques Cousteau who invented the Aqua-Lung (scuba tank). *Dolphin Log* offers that and much more, including fun science facts and regular art and writing contests for its readers. A subscription costs $15 for six issues a year.

*Highlights for Children

Ages 2–12
Write: 803 Church Street
Honesdale, PA 18431
Call: Kent Brown, Editor
Main: 717-253-1080
Fax: 717-253-0179

This magazine offers kids stories, history and nature features, and cartoons. A subscription costs $29.64 for twelve issues a year.

Submit letters as well as your poems and stories shorter than 200 words. Also send jokes and riddles (whether you made them up or heard them elsewhere) and art in either color or black-and-white. Use unlined white or solid-colored paper. Keep a copy, because nothing will be returned. Include your name, complete address, and age. There's no payment for publication.

My House

This is the house where I live.
This is where I run and play tag with my brother.
This is where my dog chases our cat around the yard.
This is where I sleep, eat, and play with my friends.
And you can hear Fritz barking,

And see all the bushes.
And feel the freshly cut grass—
And know somebody cares.

By Scott Kendall, age 10, Clovis, New Mexico. Courtesy of
Highlights for Children.

*Ink Blot

Ages 10–12
Write: Ink Blot
Attn: Margaret Larkin, Editor
7180 McCliggott Road
Saginaw, MI 48609

Ink Blot is a monthly, six-page, photocopied newsletter "designed to provide an outlet for the creative talents of those wishing to contribute." In particular, it lets writers get a byline, which means getting your name in print as the author of an article, something all novice writers are eager to obtain. Although subscriptions are not available, sample issues may be purchased for $1 each.

The newsletter accepts articles and short stories (up to one page). Short fillers (little blurbs the editors can use to fill awkward spaces in the newsletter) of twenty-five to seventy-five words are especially wanted. Poetry up to fifty lines and small black-and-white artwork are also accepted. Payment for publication is a copy of that issue *if* you send along a SASE.

*KidPub

E-mail: KidPub@KidPub.Org
Internet: http://www.kidpub.org/kidpub

KidPub is a corner of the Web where students may publish stories and news about their schools and towns. It began as an outlet for stories by the prolific, nine-year-old daughter of a Massachusetts electronics engineer. Now that KidPub accepts stories from all students, its collection has grown to more than 10,000 from all over the planet! Classroom participation is welcome.

Submit a story by filling in the handy online form. It has boxes for your name, your story, and information about yourself (favorite food, hobbies, pets). Stories submitted this way usually appear in three days or less on KidPub. Your browser software can't handle forms? Then E-mail your story to Submissions@KidPub.org.

*Live Poets Society

All ages
E-mail: editor@linda.com
Internet: http//www.linda.com/

Just can't seem to please an editor with your verse? You can always submit your creations to the Live Poets Society. This organization exists only on the Web. "The basic philosophy of the LPS," says the editor, "is to publish the work of everyone, no strings, no fees. As you can see, we have now published the work of over 700 poets and welcome the next 700 and the next and the next . . ."

Not exactly an exclusive club, but maybe somebody will stumble onto your poem, read it, and E-mail some nice comments to you.

*The McGuffey Writer

Grades K–6
Write: McGuffey Foundation School
5128 Westgage Drive
Oxford, OH 45056
E-mail: lwoedl@aol.com

From the 1800s on, generations of Americans learned to read with *The McGuffey Reader*. The McGuffey Foundation School carries on the tradition by publishing *The McGuffey Writer,* a thirty- to forty-page magazine made up exclusively of student work. "We're looking for any creative work of young people," the editor says. Although writing is emphasized, the magazine also wants artwork and photography.

The editors believe each and every submission—and they get thousands—should be returned with a constructive comment. So be sure to enclose an SASE with your submission. Payment for publication is in copies of that issue.

Guided by an adult editorial board, students at the MFS handle the work of editing and publishing the magazine. *The McGuffey Writer* is a black-and-white, saddle-stapled publication. A subscription costs $10 for three issues a year.

*Merlyn's Pen: The National Magazines of Student Writing

Grade 6
Write: P.O. Box 910
East Greenwich, RI 02818-0910
E-mail: Merlynspen@aol.com
Internet: http://www.ids.net/~merlyn/homepage
Toll free: 800-247-2027
Main: 401-885-5175
Fax: 401-885-5222

Intended for use in the classroom as well as fun reading outside of school, this full-color, thirty-two-page magazine contains student writing and art. It comes with a teacher's guide of lesson plans based on the student writing in each issue.

Submission guidelines are outlined on a full page near the front of each issue. Students pay $2 to submit up to three works, or $5 if they or their school is not a subscriber to *Merlyn's Pen*. A subscription costs $21.95 for four issues a year. Payment for publication is three copies of that issue, plus $10 for works smaller than a magazine page and $25 for works larger than a magazine page. Cover art receives $25.

Jessica let out a deep sigh. "None of you seem to have any clue who my new boyfriend is." She looked at Tracy meaningfully. "So I guess I'll have to tell you who he is."

Jessica took another deep breath. After a few seconds she let it out, and as her breath escaped, she said the name: "Daniel."

"Daniel!" Cassie shrieked. "I should've known!"

"You lover-girl, you," Lisa cooed.

"I can't believe it!" burbled Candice.

"Neither can I!" said Tracy, although she could. It was just the kind of thing you were supposed to say in this situation.

"Don't you think he's cute?" Jessica asked.

"I dare you to kiss him right in the middle of PE," Lisa giggled.

"Just go like this!" said Cassie, puckering up and making kissing noises. "Oh, Daniel . . . Daniel . . . this is so sudden!"

Excerpt from "Unwelcome Guests" by Katie Dimmery, grade 6, Matthews, North Carolina. Courtesy of *Merlyn's Pen*, December/January 1996.

National Geographic World

Grades 4–6
Write: National Geographic World
Seventeenth and M Street NW
Washington, DC 20036
Call: Ursula Bosseler
Main: 202-857-7321
Fax: 202-429-5712

Students contribute jokes, letters, and artwork to the "Mailbag" feature of *National Geographic World*. A subscription costs $17.95 for twelve issues a year.

Skipping Stones: A Multicultural Children's Magazine

Grades 4–6
Write: Skipping Stones

P.O. Box 3939
Eugene, OR 97403-0939
Internet: http://www.nonviolence.org/~nvweb/skipping
Call: Arun Toke, Editor
Main: 541-432-4956

Skipping Stones is an international, nonprofit children's magazine that encourages cooperation, creativity, and the celebration of cultural and environmental richness. It's a wonderful way for children from different lands and backgrounds to share ideas and experiences. A subscription costs $20 for individuals and $35 for schools for five issues a year.

Readers submit art, photographs, poetry, and fiction—even scenes from plays. Payment for publication is a free copy of that issue.

> *It was a sunny day at my grandmother's lake house, near Rio de Janeiro. I was playing in the water with my friends, my little sister, and my grandmother. When my mother was not watching, we all jumped from the bridge. When we fell in the water, it made a splash! . . .*
>
> *When it was getting dark and cold, we went back to the house. When I got there, I was shivering. My grandmother said, "Don't worry, you will soon be warm again." But I did not get warm. . . .*
>
> *Then she said, "I only have one more thing—a hug!" So she held me very tight. I felt warm hands squeezing me, and her beautiful voice singing a song. My heart got warm from her hug.*
>
> From "My Grandmother's Hug" by Renata Mascarenhas, age 8, Salvador, Brazil. Courtesy of *Skipping Stones*, January 1997.

*Stone Soup: the magazine by young writers and artists

Up to age 12
Write: Children's Art Foundation
P.O. Box 83

Santa Cruz, CA 95063
E-mail: editor@stonesoup.com
Internet: http://www.stonesoup.com/
Call: Ms. Gerry Mandel, Editor
Toll free: 800-447-4569
Main: 408-426-5557
Fax: 408-426-1161

"Send us writing and art about the things you feel most strongly about!" urge the editors. They want work with depth and a sense of reality, whether it's about imaginary situations or real ones.

Poems, stories, book reviews, and art are wanted. Works written in languages other than English will be considered. Don't send the same work to other magazines at the same time. All submissions must be accompanied by an SASE.

Payment for publication is a certificate, two copies of that issue, and discounts on additional copies. (A subscription regularly costs $26 for five issues a year.) In addition, $10 is paid to the creators of stories, poems, and art. Book reviewers earn $15. Illustrators earn $8. The cover artist is paid $25.

> *Remember running through the sprinkler with your baby sister? Or playing tag until the sun dipped behind the rooftops? Or both of you trying to curl up in your dad's lap for a bedtime story? Whatever it is, you remember being together, always playing tic-tac-toe, or pattycake, you were inseparable.*
>
> *Well, it was never like that for me because I didn't even know my sister until I was nine. We never curled up in our dad's lap together because we didn't have the same dad. For Michelle and me, our memories start with the end of childhood, when I was going into junior high and she into the fifth grade. At first we only saw each other when her mom and my dad had dinner together. Now, our parents are married, and day by day, week by week, we've grown to be a part of each other.*

*Teen Voices

Age 12
Write: 316 Huntington Avenue
Boston, MA 02115
Call: Katina Paron, Submission Director
Main: 617-262-2434
Fax: 617-262-8937

Only teenage girls (twelve to eighteen years old) may contribute to this magazine, created as an alternative to popular teen fashion magazines in order to address the real issues that girls deal with growing up. There are no fashion or makeup articles. A subscription costs $20 for four issues a year.

The editors welcome fiction, nonfiction, and poetry. There is no payment.

*Word Dance

Grades K–6
Write: P.O. Box 10804
Wilmington, DE 19850
Call: Stuart Ungar, Editor
Main: 302-322-6699

Word Dance looks for high-quality art and writing. Writing must be three pages or fewer. Teachers should send no more than ten submissions per class. Students may also submit items on their own. Regular sections include letters, "World Word" (what you think of our planet), "Field Trip" (about places you've visited), "Haiku Corner," and "Grab Bag" (anything goes!). The magazine is published on nonglossy paper in two colors. A subscription costs $18 for four issues per year.

Autumn

Wintry autumn
Robins, blackbirds, crows fly high
Squirrels scurry for nuts
> By Erin Semagin-Damio, grade 4,
> Mansfield, Connecticut. Courtesy
> of Word Dance, winter 1997.

Pumpkins

The orange pumpkins
Glittering in the darkness
Of the scary nights
> By Katie Coble, grade 4,
> Mansfield, Connecticut.
> Courtesy of Word Dance,
> winter 1997.

*Writer's Gallery

All ages
Write: 3240 Sylvaner Circle
Santa Cruz, CA 95062
E-mail: mikee@onestep.com
Internet: http://www.onestep.com/writers/
Call: Michael G. Crawford, Chief Editor
Main: 408-464-8827
Fax: 408-464-8817

The Writer's Gallery is a Web site. It was formed as a project to encourage new writers to finish their work, allow others to read and comment on it, and improve their skills as well as the work they have already created. The Writer's Gallery offers novels, short stories, essays, and poetry from new writers of all ages.

"I would love to have kids of all ages feel they can write—and someone cares about it," Michael Crawford says. "In fact, I'd love to have a K–6 section. Time will tell." The best way to make sure it happens is for you to submit your writing!

Submission of work for the Writer's Gallery is made via E-mail. The Writer's Gallery is listed in the *Writer's Market,* a well-known guide to writers looking for resources to aid them in improving skills or finding freelance work or publishers.

If you don't have Internet access at home, try to go online at your school or library.

*The Writers' Home Page

All ages
Write: The Writers' Home Page
528 North Bloodworth
Raleigh, NC 27604
E-mail: jacobs@rtpnet.org
Internet: http://rtpnet.org.net/~jacobs/

"Warning: This is not a E-zine," the creator says. He describes it as more like a huge bulletin board where anyone can staple something up.

Send in your poems, short stories, essays, books in progress, witticisms, and anything else that might liven up this Web site. It doesn't give prizes or run competitions. All it does is post things people send in. A section called "The Next Generations" is devoted to writers in high school and lower grades. People may write about anything so long as it's not libelous (a falsehood intended to harm someone's reputation). Submit by E-mail.

*The Writers' Slate

Grades K–6
Write: The Writing Conference
P.O. Box 664

Ottawa, KS 66067
E-mail: witeconf@idir.net
Internet: http://ecuvax.cis.ecu.edu/~engoodso/Slate.html

This journal publishes student poetry, essays, short stories—even plays. The editors are looking for "quality writing at all levels." There are three issues a year. One features the winning works from the Writing Conference's contests. Students pay $10 for subscriptions.

*Writing!

Grade 6
Write: General Learning Communications
900 Skokie Boulevard, Suite 200
Northbrook, IL 60062-4028
Call: Alan Lenhoff, Editor
Main: 847-205-3000
Fax: 847-564-8197

Writing! wants poems, essays, prose, and photos for its "Student Writing" section. It also sponsors an annual essay- and story-writing contest (see chapter 2, section "Essay," under "*Writing!* Contests").

Teachers subscribe to the twenty-four-page, full-color magazine by calling Weekly Reader Corporation at 800-446-3355. (GLC handles the editorial side only.) A subscription costs $8 for seven issues during the school year. Minimum order is fifteen subscriptions per classroom.

*Young Voices

Grades K–6
Write: P.O. Box 2321
Olympia, WA 98507
E-mail: patcha@olywa.net

Call: Steve Charak, Director
Main: 360-357-4683

Young Voices publishes six issues per year (subscription price is $20). The editor wants poems, essays, book reviews, stories, letters, and black-and-white photos and drawings. Send a query letter to find out what the editor needs currently. Enclose an SASE. Payment for use is $5 to $10.

5

Quantum Kids

Computers, Mathematics, and Science

Admit it: You are more comfortable with a transistor or a test tube than with a trombone, a tripod, a typewriter, or tap shoes. Here's where to find events to test your logic, problem-solving skills, and science know-how.

Some of these contests require a registration fee and a teacher who is willing to set aside time to involve your entire class in the event. You should find out if your school offers events that interest you. If not, you or your parents will need to persuade some school officials to give the event a try.

Computers and Mathematics

Computer Learning Month Competitions

Grades K–6
Write: Computer Learning Foundation

P.O. Box 60007
Palo Alto, CA 94306-0007
Internet: http://www.computerlearning.org/
Main: 415-327-3347
Fax: 415-327-3349

Every October is Computer Learning Month, a time for celebrating how computers are changing our lives, for learning to use new technologies, and for sharing that knowledge.

The Computer Learning Foundation offers several contests each year. It awards prizes to the individual winners and to the schools they attend.

Would you believe that you can win without having a computer or even knowing how to use one? That's right, and for a good reason. CLF doesn't want to discriminate against students without access to a computer. After all, the foundation's goal is to encourage more schools to use this technology as well as recognize those that already do.

In 1996 CLF sponsored an art contest. Students could use anything from crayons to computer software to make a poster with the theme "Using the Internet Responsibly." Another contest was the Our Town project. Teams of students and others had till April to create a Web site, not just for their school but for their community.

Prizes consist of lots of major-brand computer hardware and software goodies. There are prizes for the winners and the winners' schools. Home-school students who win get to choose a nonprofit entity to receive the school prize.

Details of the contests for an upcoming Computer Learning Month are available in August in the once-a-year publication by the Computer Learning Foundation called (what else?) *Computer Learning.*

🍎 Continental Mathematics League Contests

Write: P.O. Box 2196
St. James, NY 11780-0605

Call: Joseph Quartararo, President
Direct: 516-584-2016

This organization stages contests and olympiads in six different fields of study (see chapter 6, under section "Current Events," for the rest). These competitions consist of a series of timed examinations held over the course of the school year. Since these "meets" are conducted and graded at each school, no travel is required.

Schools apply by early October to participate. Talk to your teacher about getting involved. The fee a school pays entitles it to enter a "team" of as many students as it wants in all of a given competition's meets. However, students in different grades are regarded as being on separate teams, even if CML gives those grades the same examination. Schools pay a fee for each additional team.

Students work individually. The best individual scores are added to yield the team score. Student and team scores are sent to CML for national ranking. For the best team scores in the nation, schools receive certificates and team members receive medallions. And for every registered team, schools receive a number of certificates, ribbons, or medals to distribute to team members.

1. CONTINENTAL MATHEMATICS LEAGUE

Grades 2–6

Second and third graders take part in three meets. These consist of six questions to be answered within thirty minutes. Cost is $55 per team.

Fourth through sixth graders participate in five meets. Cost is $65 for the first team and $55 for each additional one.

Sample Question in the Third Grade

A cow has four legs and two ears. If the difference between the number of legs and the number of ears is forty, then how many cows are in the field?

2. NATIONAL SCIENCE OLYMPIAD

Grades 2–6

This competition consists of one meet lasting thirty-five minutes, to be held in late April. Schools pay $65 to register two teams, and $30 for each additional. The exam for second graders has twenty-five questions. The exam for third and fourth graders has thirty-five questions. The exam for fifth and sixth graders has forty questions.

Sample Question in the Third and Fourth Grades

The brain is part of the _____
A. nervous system   B. excretory system   C. digestive system
D. respiratory system

🍎 CyberFair: Share and Unite

Grades K–6
Write: Global SchoolNet Foundation
7040 Avenida Encinas, Suite 104-281
Carlsbad, CA 92009
E-mail: helper@gsn.org
Internet: http://www.gsn.org/
Call: Yvonne Andres
Main: 619-721-2972
Fax: 619-721-2930

The Global SchoolNet Foundation is an excellent resource for students and teachers wishing to bring technology into the classroom. Its annual contest asks schools to undertake projects to create educational Web sites.

Winners in 1996 included schools from California, Florida, Georgia, Hawaii, Maine, Massachusetts, New Mexico, North Carolina, Ohio, Texas, Virginia, and Wyoming. Additional winning entries came from schools in Australia, Bermuda, Canada, Italy, Japan, South Africa, and Sweden.

CyberKids/CyberTeens International Writing and Art Contest

Ages 7–12
Write: Mountain Lake Software *(See page 8 for contact and other information about the contest.)*

This contest has a category for games and puzzles that can be published on the World Wide Web. Possibilities include crosswords, word searches, hidden pictures, computer games, and more.

Deadline for receipt of entries is the end of the year. Voting runs through the middle of March. Prizes have included an Apple Power Macintosh, WACOM graphics tablets, cash, software, and books.

International Math Olympics

Grades K–6
Write: Youth Net
8802 San Antonio Drive
Buena Park, CA 90620
E-mail: jemartin@wviz.org (Jerry Martin)
Internet: http://youth.net/math.oly/mo.html

This contest, held during May, requires use of Speedway Math and Number Munchers, two software titles widely used in schools. You can find information about the software at http://www.mecc.com/, the Web site of its maker, Minnesota Educational Computing Corporation.

Students may compete in class or while supervised by a parent at home. Warm-up competitions are held in October, December, February, and April.

Each student competes against the software for a score. The top three scorers in each age range, as well as the top three classes (with the highest average scores), are awarded certificates, ribbons, software, and Internet announcement.

Send E-mail or snail-mail to Jerry Martin to register. Include the name of your school, a contact, the contact's E-mail or postal address, the number of students who will compete, and the students' grade levels. See the Web page for full details.

🍎The Math & Logic Contests

Grades 2–6
Write: Mike Coulter Publications
1301 NE Coronado
Lee's Summit, MO 64086
E-mail: coult@aol.com
Internet: http://www.members.com/coult/mcp.html
Main/Fax: 816-525-6195

When it comes to math, three heads are definitely better than one! These contests let you form a team of three kids to solve math problems. Your first challenge is to make sure your teacher knows about this contest and lets your class join the excitement! During the 1996–97 school year, 15,000 students from twenty states participated.

Contests for grades 2 and 3 are a two-day event in February. Those for grades 4 to 6 are a series of five events held in October, November, January, February, and March. The cost is $24.50 for a school's second or third grade, and $57.50 for the fourth, fifth, or sixth grades. A discount of 10 percent is given to schools that enter more than one grade level.

At each event, your team gets forty minutes to tackle puzzles, story problems, and problems involving money, patterns, geometry, and number concepts. Your teacher sends your school's top three team scores to Mike Coulter Publications.

After every monthly contest, members of schools' top three teams receive certificates. After the last contest of the year, additional certificates are presented to the top teams from each grade level in their geographic region and in the country as a whole. Nine trophies per grade level may be purchased for an additional $40.

Sample Questions in the Fourth Grade Contest

1. Pepsi is on sale at three different stores. Mark's Market is selling six cans for $2.99. Gary's Grocery's price is $4.99 for a twelve-pack. Fred's Foods is selling Pepsi at $10.99 for a case of 24 cans. Which store has the lowest price per can?

2. A recipe for cookies calls for 1½ cups of sugar to make 5 dozen cookies. A 5-pound bag of sugar contains 10 cups of sugar. David and Beth are making cookies for a party for their entire school. How many 5-pound bags of sugar should they buy to have enough to make 2,400 cookies?

Math League Contests

Grades 4–6
Write: Math League Press
P.O. Box 720
Tenafly, NJ 07670-0720
Internet: http://www.mathleague.com/
Call: Daniel Flegler, Director
Main: 201-568-6328
Fax: 201-816-0125

State mathematics leagues use tests created by the Math League Press to hold annual contests. Conducted in school, the contests consist of a half-hour multiple-choice exam. Calculators are permitted.

To participate, schools pay $25 per contest. They receive contest materials for grades 4 and 5 by April 1, and for grade 6 by the last Tuesday in February. Contest materials include thirty copies of the exam for each contest entered. Schools may make additional copies as necessary. And they may make special arrangements for blind or other handicapped students, or for non-English-speaking students.

In each school, the highest-scoring students in the grade 4 and grade 5 contests receive book awards. Each school's highest-scoring student in the grade 6 contest receives a certificate of merit. Additional awards are given at the county and national level.

Sample Question in the Fifth Grade Test

1. A certain bird flies south. If it flies 120 km each day and it flies 3,000 km in all, how many days does it take to make the trip?
   A. 120   B. 50   C. 25   D. 15

2. $(7 \times 15) - (7 + 14 + 21 + 28) = 7 \times$ __?
   A. 0   B. 1   C. 3   D. 5

🍎 Mathematical Olympiads for Elementary and Middle Schools

Grades 4–6
Write: 2154 Bellmore Avenue
Bellmore, NY 11710-5645
Call: Richard Kalman, Executive Director
E-mail: moes@i-2000.com
Main: 516-781-2400
Fax: 516-785-6640

This contest is held in every state and twenty-five foreign countries. Over 100,000 students participate. The organizers try to make it as easy as possible for a teacher to administer the contest.

Individual schools join the Mathematical Olympiads organization for a $75 fee ($100 for non-U.S. schools). Membership entitles schools to field a team of up to thirty-five students in the five olympiads held each year. Schools can field more teams by paying an additional fee for each.

The fee covers everything: the contest materials, copies of solutions and questions for the previous two years for teaching purposes, assorted awards for 50 percent of all students and 20 percent of all teams, and eight newsletters per year designed to walk the teacher through all the procedures.

An olympiad is a math exam consisting of five challenging problems to be solved in a limited time. Students take the exam at their own school. Awards are given after the final olympiad of the year. All participants receive a certificate. Students can also win patches, trophies, pins, and medallions based on individual performance. Schools can win a plaque and certificates based on team scores.

Sample Questions

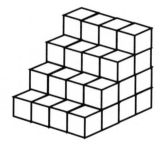

1. The stairway is made by placing identical cubes on top of each other. Not all cubes are visible. How many cubes does this stairway contain. (Time: four minutes)

2. The average weight of a group of children is 100 pounds. Todd, who weighs 112 pounds, then joins the group. This raises the average weight of the group to 102 pounds. How many children were in the original group? (Time: five minutes)

MathMagic

Grades K–6
Write: MathMagic Foundation

P.O. Box 27205
El Paso, TX 79926-7205
E-mail: alanh@laguna.epcc.edu
Internet: http://forum.swarthmore.edu/mathmagic/what.html
Call: Alan Hodson
Fax: 915-533-2902

Do you like teamwork? MathMagic was developed to motivate students to use computer technology while boosting their problem-solving and communication skills. A registered team of students pairs up with another team via the Internet and engages in a dialogue to solve a problem posted by MathMagic. When an agreement is reached, the pair posts its solution. New challenges are posted every five weeks to the student team's E-mail account (managed by a faculty sponsor). Communication between the teams in a pair is highly valued by the judges. There are no awards.

Sample Question in the Advanced Level for Kindergarten through Third Grades

Cindy is riding on an elevator in a building that has many floors and one basement floor underground. Answer these questions regarding Cindy's adventure riding the elevator up and down the building.

1. From the first floor, Cindy goes up eight floors and then down three floors. What floor is she now on?

2. Cindy is on the eighteenth floor. She goes down ten floors and then up thirteen floors. What floor is she now on?

3. Cindy is on the seventh floor. She then goes up to the nineteenth floor. How many floors did she go up?

4. Cindy is on the second floor. She goes down three floors. What floor is she now on?

🍎 National Mathematics League Competitions

Grade 6
Write: National Mathematics League
P.O. Box 9459
Coral Springs, FL 33075
Call: Diane Riley
Main: 954-344-8980
Fax: 954-752-1424

Schools that register with NML administer a series of five tests to their students from January to April. There are calculus and precalculus divisions open to all interested students. But algebra II, geometry, algebra I, prealgebra, and sixth-grade math are open only to students currently enrolled in those courses.

Schools register by the end of October. The fee is $55 for the first division and $40 for each additional. Each school receives a rosette ribbon to award to its first- and second-place students in each division. The top schools in each division receive a plaque.

🍎 National TIVY Tournament

Grades 1–6
Write: TIVY Games
4341 Will Rogers Parkway
Oklahoma City, OK 73108
Call: Bernie McGowan, President
Toll free: 800-922-8489
Main: 405-946-9706
Fax: 405-946-8489

Entrepreneur Bernie McGowan was concerned about the increasingly poor math skills among his newly hired employees. He saw the need for a fun way to sharpen students' math skills. So he developed TIVY, a checkerslike board game in which players try to create the highest-scoring math problem and then solve it.

Oklahoma City schools put TIVY in their classrooms and then carefully analyzed the results. They found that TIVY users significantly outperformed nonusers on standardized tests.

TIVY is used in every state, but so far only schools in Toledo, Ohio, and Oklahoma City use the game heavily.

The manufacturer says that acceptance continues to grow for TIVY as a noncurricular way to boost student interest and ability in math. Over 500 students participated in the national tournament in Oklahoma in May 1996. Call the company to find out how to get TIVY in your school.

🍎 24 Challenge®

Grades 4–6
Write: Suntex International
118 North Third Street
Easton, PA 18042
E-mail: Math24@aol.com
Call: Xantha Calsetta, Program Coordinator
Main: 610-253-5255
Fax: 610-258-2180

Your brain is faster than a calculator, and the 24 Challenge Math Program proves it. The challenge is a tournament-style activity based on the 24 game. Students gather around, and a 24 card is turned up. On each card is printed four numbers. Students race mentally to use each number once in a calculation that equals 24. For instance, a card might have the numbers 2, 4, 8, and 8. Solution: $2 \times 4 = 8$. Then, $8 + 8 + 8 = 24$.

There are three degrees of difficulty. The more difficult the card, the more points you get for solving it first. There are also nine different editions of the 24 game. Advanced versions incorporate fractions, decimals, exponents, and algebra.

In the United States alone, 100,000 classrooms with 3 million students play this game. It is used in South Africa, New Zealand, and in all Dutch elementary schools. Belgium, Portugal, and the United Kingdom recently joined in. A study in Erie, Pennsylvania, found that using the 24 game for five to ten minutes as part of the daily math curriculum can boost standardized math scores by as much as sixty percentile points. Call the company to find out how to get the game in your school.

Science

Fire-Fighting Home Robot Contest

All ages
Write: Connecticut Robotics Society
190 Mohegan Drive
West Hartford, CT 06117
E-mail: JMENDEL141@aol.com
Internet: http://shakti.trincoll.edu/~jhough/fire_robot/
Call: Jake Mendelssohn
Direct: 860-233-2379
Fax: 860-232-0435

Students go head to head with NASA scientists and university professors in this contest. The robots they build must be computer-controlled (as opposed to using remote control). They must race through a maze that represents a four-room house, detect a lit candle, and extinguish it with air, foam, or by other nondangerous means. And the robot must really find the candle; it can't just flood the house with CO_2 and put it out accidentally.

The contest is held in late April at Trinity College in Connecticut. There is a separate division for students in high school and below, with a prize of $1,000. Can students that young really "do robotics" without the help of an adult? "Usually the adults hold them back," says Professor Jake Mendelssohn. In the 1996 contest, a fourth-grade girl and her seventh-grade brother entered a robot that outperformed one created by a team of three MIT professors.

International BEAM Web Games

All ages
Write: Mark Tilden
Mail Stop D454
LANL
Los Alamos, NM 87545
E-mail: mwtilden@lanl.gov
Internet: http://sst.lanl.gov/robot/
Call: Mark Tilden, Organizer
Direct: 505-667-2902
Fax: 505-665-3644

People near and far might have learned about past versions of BEAM (Biology, Electronics, Aesthetics, and Mechanics), a robot-building competition, on the World Wide Web. In the past the "near" could easily compete, but the "far" often couldn't. That's all changed. Now you don't have to bring your robot to New Mexico; you just mail it. The organizers promise to let it compete in a fair match. You get to watch a video of the match that the organizers will post on the Web site!

Since you won't be there, who will operate the radio controls? No one! These robots can't be "radio-controlled puppets" but must truly be self-guided. Believe it or not, you could probably build one out of some broken toys and miscellaneous techno-junk lying around your house. "Bizarre ideas are encouraged," the organizers say.

All the events are nondestructive. They include Solar Roller, Photo-Vore, and Walking. One year a robot built by a seven-year-old girl beat the complicated, etched titanium creation of an MIT professor!

The contest is held in the spring. Check the Web site for contest details, where to get robot kits and parts, technical instructions, and more.

Invent America!

Grades K–6
Write: United States Patent Model Foundation
1505 Powhatan Street
Alexandria, VA 22314
Main: 703-684-1836

Invent America! was created for use in schools. But community groups and individual parents may participate by ordering the enrollment kit for $15. The program guides you through finding a problem that could be solved with an invention, to creating and constructing a solution. Students' inventions can be submitted to the national Invent America! contest. Prizes are U.S. Savings Bonds worth $1,000, $500, $250, and $100 for each grade division.

Inventors Workshop International Education Foundation Events

Write: Inventors Workshop International Education Foundation
1029 Castillo Street
Santa Barbara, CA 93101
Internet: http://www.ideahelp.com/
Call: Alan Tratner, President
Main: 805-962-5722
Fax: 805-899-4927

The IWIEF was founded to help inventors learn how to protect and develop their ideas. It sponsors a couple of great contests.

1. GREAT IDEA CONTEST™

All ages

This annual contest is open to all. Send $2.50 and a nine-by-twelve-inch SASE to get the rules. Your entry will be a three-dimensional model or poster depicting an invention. Entries are due by the end of August. Four prizes of $1,000 were awarded in previous years.

Categories include agriculture, arts, chemical, construction, education, electrical, energy, environmental, food, furniture, games, medical, recreation, tools, toys, transportation, and miscellaneous.

2. YOUNG ECO INVENTORS CONTEST

Ages 6–12

Students are invited to show concern for the environment by thinking up an eco-friendly invention. The contest takes place at Eco Expo, held each April in Los Angeles. The $1,000 grand prizes have been won by such ideas as "haz-a-meter," "recyclable house," and "heater helper." Sponsors include the IWIEF, Eco Expo, and Environmental Education Group.

Mouse Trap–Powered Vehicle Challenge

Write: Olmsted Falls Middle School
Attn: Dan Radman
27045 Bagley Road
Olmsted Falls, OH 44138
E-mail: dradma@Leeca8.Leeca.ohio.gov
Internet: http://leeca8.leeca.ohio.gov/ofcs/ms/MTPV_Files/
   mtpv.html
Call: Dan Radman, Science Teacher
Main: 216-235-8400
Fax: 216-235-7988

For this contest, you get to build a vehicle that is powered by a mousetrap instead of batteries.

First get hold of a Victor-brand mousetrap measuring one and three-quarters inches by three and seven-eighths inches. Build your vehicle out of anything, but don't use any power-assisting devices like rubber bands. Find an empty school hallway or gymnasium for a test track, arm the mousetrap, and drop a coin on the bait holder.

It's not uncommon for an MTPV to travel less than 10 feet. Better than 30 feet is a good run. Over 70 feet is excellent. A California student achieved 158 feet, 2 inches. Last time we checked, that was the world record.

Visit the Web site or send a letter to register for the competition, held during the school year and open to any student anywhere. An MTPV Hall of Fame at the Web site lists the builders of the top ten vehicles. Be sure to click on the pieces of cheese to hear cat noises.

National Science Olympiad

Look in this chapter, under Computers and Mathematics section, "Continental Mathematics League Contests."

🍎 National Science Teachers Association Contests

Write: National Science Teachers Association
1840 Wilson Boulevard
Arlington, VA 22201-3000
Internet: http://www.nsta.org/
Main: 703-243-7100
Fax: 703-243-7177

1. CRAFTSMAN/NSTA YOUNG INVENTORS AWARDS

Grades 4–6
E-mail: msnipes-austin@nsta.org

Call: Monica Snipes-Austin
Toll free: 888-494-4994

Design a new or improved tool, and you could win $10,000. Work by yourself or keep an "inventor's log" to track your progress. After you perfect your tool, submit the log along with a hand drawing of your tool and a photograph of the tool or a model of it. Clarity of communication and practicality of your invention count. Deadline is early April.

Twelve regional winners are chosen. Their inventions are compared by the national judging team. The national winner gets a $10,000 U.S. Savings Bond, while the eleven finalists get $5,000 U.S. Savings Bonds. All students who submit a complete entry receive a certificate and gift.

2. SPACE SCIENCE STUDENT INVOLVEMENT PROGRAM (SSIP)

Attn: SSIP
E-mail: ssip@nsta.org
Call: Kathlyn Berry, SSIP Director

To be eligible for SSIP contests, you must attend a U.S. school or home school, or a school for dependents of U.S. government employees overseas. There are many rules, and they must be followed to the letter, so send off for the brochure by September. Your entry must be postmarked early the following January.

SSIP Future Aircraft/Spacecraft Design Competition

Grades 3–5

Some authors of 1930s science fiction wrote of huge aircraft with fifty propellers on each wing! They failed to foresee the replacement of propellers with jet engines. What's your guess for the future? Will we still be buckling our seat belts? Or will transportation have evolved into a space suit that enables travel through quantum tunnels in space, instantly bringing us to our destination with no need for in-flight snacks?

Your team of at least three members must work that one out. If your idea best pleases the judges, you take a trip (sorry, by conventional means only) to NASA's Space Camp. You and an adviser also are brought to the National Space Science Symposium in Washington, D.C.

Use your own ideas. Don't borrow concepts like *Star Trek*'s Transporter Room. Create three images of your craft: a complete exterior view, a schematic (blueprint or floor plan) of the interior, and a detail of any special function you wish to highlight. These images should be eight and a half by eleven inches, created with traditional art tools and supplies.

You also need to write up to 1,000 words describing your vehicle and explaining how your team arrived at its design concept. Detail its type, size, shape, construction materials, destination, mission, and value to humankind. For instance, will it allow the delivery boy to bring a pizza that's still hot?

SSIP Mission to Planet Earth

Grade 6

Satellites bring us awesome photos of hurricanes, photos that aid mapmakers, even radar-revealed images beneath the earth's surface. Spy satellites do even more amazing stuff, like eavesdrop on terrorist phone calls and photograph top-secret installations so well you can read the license plate on a car! A satellite once even detected a secret nuclear test.

The ability to gather such varied information from space could help scientists track and deal with the changes man causes to the environment. What's needed are teams of three or four students to develop a mission plan.

First you will figure out which human activity needs study soonest, given that scientific funding is always limited. Then come up with a related hypothesis and design an experiment to test it, making some use of satellites. Third, hatch a plan for the future. Keep the three-part mission plan under 1,500 words total.

3. TOSHIBA NSTA EXPLORAVISION AWARDS PROGRAM

Grades K–6
E-mail: priley@nsta.org
Call: Pamela Riley
Toll free: 800-EXPLOR-9
Direct: 703-312-9216
Fax: 703-243-7177

U.S. and Canadian students, working in teams of three or four, envision what a form of technology today (like the telephone) will be like in twenty years. Teams must submit a paper, ten pages or fewer, including illustrations, describing the past, present, and future of the technology that they have chosen. In addition to the paper, students must submit ten storyboard frames that are scenes from a videotape they may be asked to make if they are regional winners.

What are some of the prizewinning ideas from ExploraVision contests in recent years? Well, there are highways that fill their own potholes, and "smart" refrigerators that suggest recipes based on available foods. One ExploraVision team even suggested the possibility of "living" lightbulbs based on bioluminescence (think fireflies)!

Entry deadline falls in early February. Every student team member who enters the competition with a complete entry receives a certificate of participation and a small gift. Student entry certificates and gifts are sent to the teacher-adviser for distribution.

Student members of the four first-place teams each receive a $10,000 U.S. Savings Bond or Canadian savings bond of comparable issue price. Student members of the eight second-place teams each receive a $5,000 bond. The twelve finalist teams and their parents or guardians win trips to Washington, D.C., in June to attend the awards ceremony. Students on the remaining thirty-six regional winning teams each receive a $100 bond.

More than 18,000 U.S. and Canadian students in kindergarten through twelfth grade entered the 1995–96 competition.

A Pledge and A Promise Environmental Awards

Grades K–6; home schools ineligible
Write: Sea World
Education Department
7007 Sea World Drive
Orlando, FL 32821
Internet: http://www.bev.net/education/SeaWorld/Pledge/
  pledgeandpromise.html
Call: Sheila Sullivan
Main: 407-363-2389
Direct: 314-577-2622
Fax: 314-577-9977

These awards honor outstanding efforts of school groups for their lasting contributions to the environment. Possible projects include cleaning up a polluted area, recycling, monitoring the ecological health of an area, educating others on environmental issues, raising funds to buy land, and more. Projects must be creative, innovative, and primarily student-driven. They must have measurable criteria.

Finalists in 1996 carried out such projects as restoring urban waterways, restoring frog habitat, building a nature trail, and removing graffiti.

Nomination submissions must be receive by January 31. Grand prize is $20,000. All thirteen awards total $100,000.

President's Environmental Youth Awards

Grades K–6
Write: United States Environmental Protection Agency

401 M Street SW
Washington, DC 20460
Call: Doris Gillispie, Youth Program Coordinator
Main: 202-260-8749
Fax: 202-260-0790

Did you do something for the environment? Be recognized for your good deed! The ten regional EPA offices honor projects of all kinds. Those that got especially significant results can be considered in the national competition.

Examples from the past: A Girl Scout troop in Hawaii restored a pond that had been turned into a dump. FFA members in Georgia built and continue to operate a recycling center that reduced the amount of trash in the landfill by 300,000 pounds. A Boy Scout troop in New York came up with a project to prevent the erosion of valuable topsoil in their area. All participants receive certificates signed by the president of the United States, honoring them for their efforts in environmental protection. One outstanding project from each of the EPA regions is honored by EPA Headquarters in Washington, D.C.

Regional EPA offices are located in these cities and serve the following states:

Office	Telephone	States Served
Atlanta	404-347-3004	Ala., Fla., Ga., Ky., Miss., N.C., S.C., Tenn.
Boston	617-565-9447	Conn., Mass., Maine, N.H., R.I., Vt.
Chicago	312-886-0995	Ill., Ind., Mich., Minn., Ohio, Wis.
Dallas	214-655-2204	Ark., La., N.M., Okla., Tex.
Denver	303-312-5516	Colo., Mont., N. Dak., S. Dak., Utah, Wyo.
Kansas City	913-551-7003	Iowa, Kans., Mo., Nebr.
New York	212-637-3678	N.J., N.Y., P.R., V.I.
Philadelphia	215-597-6685	Del., Md., Pa., Va., W. Va., D.C.
San Francisco	415-744-1582	Ariz., Calif., Hawaii, Nev.
Seattle	206-553-0149	Alaska, Idaho, Ore., Wash.

Rube Goldberg Contest

Grades K–6
Write: Eta Kappa Nu Honor Society
Department of Electrical Engineering
University of Kentucky
453 Anderson Hall
Lexington, KY 40506-0046
E-mail: hkn@engr.uky.edu
Internet: http://www.engr.uky.edu/student.orgs/hkn/
Call: HKN President
Main: 606-257-4156

University chapters of HKN, the honor society for electrical engineering types, sponsor various contests during National Engineers Week in February. The University of Kentucky event is generally for locals but serves as an example of what might go on elsewhere. If you live near a university, call the engineering department and ask if it stages contests for students like yourself.

The Rube Goldberg Contest is named after the Pulitzer Prize–winning cartoonist whose characters used ridiculously complicated machinery to do simple, everyday tasks. The 1996 contest called for the most bizarre way to squeeze toothpaste onto a toothbrush. The winning team received a pizza party.

Science Olympiad

Grades K–6
Write: Science Olympiad
5955 Little Pine Lane
Rochester Hills, MI 48306
Call: Sharon Putz, Executive Administrator
Main: 810-651-4013
Fax: 810-651-7835

Approximately 2.5 million students from more than 13,000 schools from all fifty states participate in the Science Olympiad. (Each school pays a fee of $60 to become a member of Science Olympiad.) Students join their team almost as soon as school starts in the fall. It's not unusual for teams to practice together nights and weekends as they prepare for their local and state contests and—if they make the cuts—the national competition.

More than thirty events embrace all fields of science that require physical exertion. For instance, in the pentathlon, teams traverse five physical obstacles on a course, only to encounter "mental" obstacles as well. In another event, contestants use a catapult to hurl a tennis ball at a sand pit.

The National Finals, held in May at a different college campus each year, brings together about 2,500 students. Awards include medals, trophies, and scholarships.

Space Settlement Design Contest

Grade 6
Write: NASA Ames Research Center
Attn: Al Globus
MS T27A-1
Moffett Field, CA 94035-1000
E-mail: globus@nas.nasa.gov
Internet: http://www.nas.nasa.gov/NAS/SpaceSettlement/
Call: Al Globus
Main: 415-604-5000
Direct: 415-604-4404
Fax: 415-604-3957

Want to design a space colony? Or do you prefer to focus on a single aspect of living in space? You can do either in this contest, which encourages imaginative, artistic entries. Stories, artwork, and models are welcome.

Enter on your own or as part of a team. You don't need to travel. Mail in your design by the end of March, and that's it. In 1996 a team from Argentina won with a dazzling, inch-thick report that included pictures, text, equations, even a student-written shuttle simulator program. See that entry and a team photo at http://science.nas.nasa.gov/Services/Education/SpaceSettlement/Contest/Results/96/winner/.

First-, second-, and third-place awards are given to individuals and groups. All participants receive certificates. Winning entries are turned into NASA Web pages!

Student Technology Contest in Magnetic Levitation

Grade 6
Write: Brookhaven National Laboratory
Science Education Center
Building 438
P.O. Box 5000
Upton, NY 11973-5000
E-mail: swyler@bnl.gov
Internet: http://sun20.ccd.bnl.gov/~scied/programs/maglev.html
Call: Dr. Karl Swyler
Direct: 516-344-7171
Fax: 516-344-5832

A conventional train can travel no more than 185 mph, but a train that floats on magnets can reach 300 mph. That advantage drives the research and fuels the excitement over magnetic levitation technology.

Brookhaven, whose scientists pioneered the MagLev field, cosponsors a contest in which middle school students build tin can–sized MagLev vehicles that race on a fourteen-foot track. Participation in the contest has boomed since it began in 1989. It started in Long Island and is spreading through the Northeast. Brookhaven has prepared materials to enable others to replicate the contest elsewhere, enabling the contest to reach nationwide eventually.

🍎 Student Technology Leaders Competition

Grades K–6
Write: MultiMedia Schools
c/o Deneen Frazier
107-B West Carr Street
Carrboro, NC 27510
E-mail: deneen@mindspring.com
Call: Deneen Frazier
Main: 919-929-2913
Fax: 919-968-1561

Are you the computer whiz at your school? This award honors outstanding students who make exemplary and innovative use of information technology in their schools and communities. In the eyes of their teachers and fellow students, these kids serve as technology leaders, and the amazing projects they create and maintain prove it.

To enter the competition, you must be nominated by a teacher or school administrator. Examples of the student's work in any format are accepted but are not required. Nominations must be postmarked no later than the end of February. Don't be shy; ask your teacher to nominate you and tell why you should be.

Three students are chosen to attend the National Educational Computing Conference in Minneapolis, Minnesota, in June. At the conference, these students present their projects to the participants and receive an award. Modest and reasonable travel expenses are reimbursed for the winners and one chaperone each.

See also:
YOUNG AMERICA (chapter 7, under section "Membership Organizations")

6

Scattered Matters

Current Events, Economics, English Language Arts, French, Geography, Handwriting, History, Multidiscipline Competitions, Mythology, and Social Studies

This chapter has all the contests that didn't fit under the other categories. But watch out! It also has some multidiscipline contests. Those demand some combination of skills, such as writing, art, math, science, geography, literature, history, and more. If you like any one of those categories in particular, you should consider entering the multidiscipline contests in addition to the single-topic contests.

Some of the contests here require a modest amount of class time and/or money. You'll need to persuade your parents and teachers that these contests are worth it.

Current Events

🍎 Continental Mathematics League Contests

Write: P.O. Box 2196

St. James, NY 11780-0605
Call: Joseph Quartararo, President
Direct: 516-584-2016

This organization stages contests and olympiads in six different fields of study—not just math (see previous chapter under section "Computers and Mathematics" for the rest). These competitions consist of a series of timed examinations held over the course of the school year. Since these "meets" are conducted and graded at each school, no travel is required.

Schools apply by early October to participate. The fee a school pays entitles it to enter a "team" of as many students as it wants in all of a given competition's meets. However, students in different grades are regarded as being on separate teams, even if CML gives those grades the same examination. Schools pay a fee for each additional team.

Students work individually. The best individual scores are added to yield the team score. Student and team scores are sent to CML for national ranking. For the best team scores in the nation, schools receive certificates and team members receive medallions. And for every registered team, schools receive a number of certificates, ribbons, or medals to distribute to team members.

1. NATIONAL CURRENT EVENTS LEAGUE

Grades 4–6

Most subjects are taught in school. When it comes to current events, though, read a newspaper regularly to get the scoop.

This competition consists of four meets lasting thirty minutes. Schools pay $45 to register the first team, and $25 for each additional. The exams for all grades are at the same level, having thirty questions based on the news from the previous several months. New areas include general, arts and entertainment, health and science, business and finance, and sports.

Sample Question: Fourth through Sixth Grades

Evander Holyfield defeated Mike Tyson on November 9 to become only the second man in history to be a three-time heavyweight champion. The sport is _____.
A. boxing   B. wrestling   C. weight lifting

2. NATIONAL GEOGRAPHY OLYMPIAD

Grades 2–6

This competition consists of one meet lasting thirty-five minutes, to be held in late April. Schools pay $50 to register the first team, and $30 for each additional. The exam for grade 2 has twenty-five questions. The exam for grades 3 and 4 has thirty-five questions. The exam for grades 5 and 6 has forty questions.

Sample Question: Second Grade

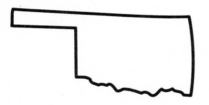

This is the state of _____.
A. Oklahoma   B. Idaho   C. Florida   D. Tennessee

3. NATIONAL LANGUAGE ARTS OLYMPIAD

Grades 2–6

This competition consists of one meet lasting thirty-five minutes, to be held in late April. Schools pay $65 to register two teams, and $30 for each additional. The exam for grade 2 has twenty-five questions. The exam for grades 3 and 4 has thirty-five questions. The exam for grades 5 and 6 has fifty questions. The questions cover spelling, vocabulary, reading comprehension, analogies, and grammar.

Sample Question: Second Grade

We use _____ to find the difference between two numbers.
A. subtracshin   B. subtrakshun   C. subtracsion   D. subtraction

4. NATIONAL SOCIAL STUDIES OLYMPIAD

Grades 2–6

This competition consists of one meet lasting thirty-five minutes, to be held in late April. Schools pay $65 to register two teams, and $30 for each additional. The exams for all grades are at the same level. The exam for grade 2 has twenty-five questions. The exam for grades 3 and 4 has thirty-five questions. The exam for grades 5 and 6 has forty questions. The questions cover North American studies, geography, and government.

Sample Question: Fifth and Sixth Grades

Which province of Canada is farthest west?
A. Alberta   B. British Columbia   C. Manitoba   D. Saskatchewan

❧Future Problem Solving Program

Grades K–6
Write: 318 West Ann Street
Ann Arbor, MI 48104-1337
E-mail: fpsolv@aol.com
Internet: http://www.fpsp.org
Main: 313-998-7377
Direct: 313-998-7876
Fax: 313-998-7663

Okay, genius, you can memorize the Bill of Rights or the value of π to ten decimal places. But can you use what you know to solve real-world problems like crime control? Find out with the Future Problem Solving Program.

Guided by a teacher-coach, you and three teammates learn the FPSP six-step process. During the school year, you tackle problems and then mail your solutions to evaluators. The topics are the same ones that stump our best scientists, economists, and politicians. Recent examples: "Firearms Control," "Cybernetics," and "the United Nations."

You sharpen your skills with your first two problems. The third problem pits your wits against those of other teams at your grade level. Top-scoring teams attend state bowls, where state champs are invited to the International Conference held in June. There, 1,600 students and coaches enjoy four days of problem solving, educational seminars, and social activities.

Most states and some countries have an FPSP affiliate director who is responsible for organizing local FPSP activities. Students living outside existing FPSP-affiliated states or areas may participate through the Open division administered by the FPSP International Office. All teams in this division that excel on the third problem are invited to the International Conference.

When you're confident of your problem-solving skills, show them off in your own neighborhood through the Community Problem Solving division. FPSP students in Massachusetts designed a wastewater plant building that saved local residents nearly $119,000.

Economics

🍎The Stock Market Game

Grades 4–6
Write: Securities Industry Foundation for Economic Education
120 Broadway, Thirty-fifth Floor
New York, NY 10271-0080
E-mail: sifee@sia.com

Internet: http://www.smg2000.org/
Call: SMG National Director
Main: 212-608-0519
Fax: 212-732-6069

Here's $100,000. Don't spend it all on video games—invest it! If you're not sure where to begin, you need the Stock Market Game (or the separate SMG2000 if your classroom has Internet access). You'll learn about the U.S. economic system, the stock market, the sources and uses of capital, and related concepts.

Some 20,000 teachers already involve their classrooms totaling 700,000 kids. Ask your teachers to sign up. Fees for the program vary by state from $5 to $25 per team, with an average of five teams per classroom. The game takes as little as one hour a week of class time.

After ten weeks the value of your team's portfolio will be compared to that of other teams in your grade and state or region. Some states use essay contests to select winners. But generally, the winners are teams whose portfolios grew in value the most. Prizes vary by state and might include plaques, luncheons, T-shirts, cash, or U.S. Savings Bonds.

English Language Arts

🍎 BOOK IT! National Reading Incentive Program

Grades K–6
Write: P.O. Box 2999
Wichita, KS 67201
E-mail: read@bookitprogram.com
Call: Marlene Cunningham
Toll free: 800-426-6548
Main: 316-687-8401
Fax: 316-687-8937

This five-month reading incentive program annually captivates 22 million students in the United States, Canada, and Australia. And no wonder—as it turns kids into bookworms, it also makes them pizza-worms!

The only requirement is that students meet their monthly reading goal. Their teacher gives them a certificate redeemable for pizza. If students meet the goals for all five months, they also get a medallion and neck ribbon. If an entire classroom meets the goals for four out of the five months, they and their teachers win a classroom pizza party.

Enrollment deadline for the program is mid-June.

National Language Arts Olympiad

Look in this chapter, under Current Events section, "Continental Mathematics League Contests."

Scripps Howard National Spelling Bee

Grades K–6
Write: Scripps Howard
P.O. Box 5380
Cincinnati, OH 45201
E-mail: bee@scripps.com
Internet: http://www.spellingbee.com/
Call: Paige Pipkin, Director, Business and Public Affairs
Main: 513-977-3040
Fax: 513-977-3019

This is the most famous contest in the United States. Nine million kids compete at the local level to spell words like *antipyretic* and *sma-*

ragdine. Some 230 local winners proceed to the national event in Washington. Here's the contest timetable:

★   **October and November.** Buy Paideia (the 3,000-word contest word list) from your local bee's local sponsor while supplies last. Some local sponsors may use a different list. You can find your sponsor's name at the Web site, or call or write to Scripps Howard. *Note:* Two major areas—Seattle, Washington, and Austin, Texas—are unsponsored. Students there have no way to compete.

★   **January through March.** Preliminaries are held in classrooms.

★   **March and April.** Semifinals determine local winners, who will advance to national finals.

★   **Late May through early June.** Local sponsors pay for travel, hotel, and meals for the local winners and an adult escort to attend the National Spelling Bee for a week. Barbecues, ice cream socials, sight-seeing, and a spelling bee for parents take up Sunday through Tuesday. The National Spelling Bee is Wednesday and Thursday. More parties, tours, and an awards banquet follow on Friday.

The national champ pockets $5,000 cash, a $1,000 U.S. Savings Bond, and more. Other finalists receive from $50 to $4,000.

Vocabulary University℠

Grades 4–6
Write: P.O. Box 7727
Menlo Park, CA 94026
E-mail: rich@syndicate.com
Internet: http://www.vocabulary.com/
Call: Carey Orr Cook
Main/Fax: 415-854-9698

You will never earn a degree faster than at Vocabulary University, a Web site where you have fun while learning new words.

Participation is free. When you first visit Vocabulary University, fill in the simple registration form. That way, a computer will keep track of the word puzzles you complete each time you visit.

Each set of puzzles teaches twelve words. Clues are provided. After you submit a form with your answers, you instantly see another form with your answers, the correct answers, and the words used in a sentence.

Once you finish twelve sets of puzzles, you receive a colorful "degree." T-shirts, achievement pins, and other awards go to students who complete all three of Vocabulary University's teaching levels: high elementary, junior high/middle school, and high school/college prep.

If you enjoy these word puzzles, you can find more at the sister Web site http://www.syndicate.com/. There you have a chance to win $10 gift certificates for Blockbuster Video.

Sample Puzzle for High Elementary

Find four words based on the root *spect,* meaning "to look at or examine." Example: *spectator.*

1. Ten-letter noun beginning with i. Official examination or review; the act of examining carefully and critically, especially for flaws.

2. Eight-letter noun beginning with *p.* Something expected; possibility; a potential customer or purchaser.

3. Seven-letter verb beginning with s. To have doubts about; to distrust; to surmise to be true or probable.

4. Nine-letter noun beginning with s. A public performance or display; something seen or capable of being seen.

❦WordMasters Challenge

Grades 3–6
Write: WordMasters
213 East Allendale Avenue
Allendale, NJ 07401
Main: 201-327-4201
Fax: 201-327-6219

This national contest encourages growth in vocabulary and verbal reasoning. To excel, students must master the meanings of words and be able to reason out the relationships between words.

Teachers should enroll their classes by mid-October. For a fee of $55 per grade level (some discounts are available), your class will participate in three "analogies meets" in December, February, and April. At each grade level there is a Blue division for average students and a Gold division for those of superior abilities.

The top ten scores from a classroom become the team score, which is forwarded to WordMasters for national ranking. The highest-scoring students in each class receive medals and certificates at the end of the year.

Sample Analogy for the Third Grade

SNOW : WHITE :: BLOOD: _____
(vein / warm / flowing / scarlet / ice)

Sample Analogy for the Sixth Grade

FIELD : FALLOW :: _____
(hiker : laden / ditch : deep / factor: idle / cellar : dark / squabble: angry)

French

National French Contest (Le Grand Concours)

Grades K–6
Write: American Association of Teachers of French
Le Grand Concours
P.O. Box 32030
Sarasota, FL 34239
Internet: http://www.utsa.edu/aatf/aatf.html
Call: Sidney Teitelbaum, Director
Fax: 941-364-9820

This test is open to all students of French in a U.S. school, students on overseas campuses, those with tutors, and home schoolers. Some 75,000 students in kindergarten through twelfth grades take the exam each March.

Cost is based on a kit that contains materials to test twenty students. Form A (speaking and listening comprehension) costs $25. Form B adds reading comprehension and costs $27. Individual exams may be ordered for a few dollars each.

All participants receive Certificats de Mérite. The top 20 percent in each AATF chapter receive Certificats d'Honneur. The best students nationwide receive Certificats Lauréat National. The top eight students nationally in every division and level receive gold, silver, or bronze medals.

Geography

National Geography Bee

Grades 4–6
Write: National Geographic Society
1145 Seventeenth Street NW
Washington, DC 20036-4688

Call: Lori Saylor, National Geography Bee
Main: 202-828-6659
Direct: 202-828-5455
Fax: 202-857-7159

Want to know what this contest is like? See for yourself. Most PBS stations broadcast the national finals in late May. The moderator for almost a decade has been Alex Trebek, host of the TV game show *Jeopardy!*

The competition is also open to students through the eighth grade. Don't worry—more than a third of the finalists in 1996 were age twelve or under. Principals register their schools to participate by October 15. (Home schools also participate. Some home schoolers were finalists in 1995 and 1996.) Cost is $20.

A school competition, consisting of written and oral questions, is held sometime in December or early January. The school champions then take a written test to qualify for their state bees. The top 100 students in a state go to their state bee, a fun, high-publicity event that is often held in the state capital. The state bees are oral and written tests in early spring.

Finally, the top finalist from each of the fifty states and seven U.S. territories—out of the 5 million students who began the bee— compete in the national finals in late May. Prizes total $50,000, including a $25,000 scholarship for first place.

Sample Questions

1.   Where would you travel to search for the Loch Ness Monster, visit Edinburgh Castle, and watch the Highland Games— Scotland or Bulgaria?

2.   The cave system thought to be the world's longest is in which Appalachian state?

3.   Poland, France, and Denmark all border what country?

National Geography Olympiad

Look in this chapter, under Current Events section, "Continental Mathematics League Contests."

Handwriting

The National Cursive Handwriting Contest

Grades 3–6
Write: Peterson Directed Handwriting
P.O. Box 249
315 South Maple Avenue
Greensburg, PA 15601-0249
E-mail: mrpencil@pgh.net
Internet: http://www.cyberburg.com/peterson
Main: 412-837-4900
Fax: 412-836-4110

This contest gives kids with good handwriting the chance to earn membership in an honor society and a prize, too!

Any student, including home schoolers, may enter for a fifty-cent fee. Request information anytime from Peterson Directed Handwriting. The company, a publisher of education materials, sends out the contest materials in the fall. Deadline for entry is always March 15.

All participants receive a certificate. Handwriting that shows superior skill earns you a place in that year's National Cursive Handwriting Honor Society, which comes with a membership certificate. This roster of students (and their teachers) is sent to participating schools.

In addition, a champion is named for each grade level. Those students win $50 U.S. Savings Bonds.

The National Handwriting Contest

Grades 1–6
Write: Zaner-Bloser
P.O. Box 16764
Columbus, OH 43216-6764

E-mail: zanerblose@aol.com
Call: Richard Northup
Toll free: 800-421-3018
Fax: 614-487-2699

Do you always dot your *i*'s and cross your *t*'s? Then this is the contest for you!

To enter, your school or home school must teach handwriting using materials from Zaner-Bloser, a textbook publisher. It doesn't matter how long ago a school bought the materials. Similarly, a home school that had purchased a single Zaner-Bloser handwriting workbook would qualify.

Contact Zaner-Bloser anytime to be added to the contest mailing list. The company sends out the contest materials in October. Schools conduct the contest for their students. Grades 1 and 2 compete in manuscript style (printing), while grades 3 to 6 compete in cursive style (handwriting). In 1997 more than 100,000 students entered the contest from Canada, the fifty states, and Puerto Rico.

Schools select one winner from each grade and send those entries to Zaner-Bloser by the annual March 1 deadline. Judges select state/ province winners for each grade (as long as a state's entries are good enough). Those students and their schools receive a certificate and possibly another prize. (In 1997 it was a Parker pen.)

The judges then select a single winner for each grade. Those six students receive a plaque and $500 U.S. Savings Bond. Their parents, teacher, school principal, and classmates all get T-shirts.

Finally, a grand champion is selected from among the six grade-level winners. That student receives an additional $500 bond and plaque.

History

American History Essay Contest

Grades 5–6; "sanctioned" home schools eligible
Write: National Society Daughters of the American Revolution

1776 D Street NW
Washington, DC 20006-5392
Main: 202-879-3253
Fax: 202-879-3252

Historians are long-range detectives. They try to shed light on serious issues, and even not-so-serious but nonetheless controversial ones such as whether George Washington wore false teeth made of wood. No telling what you may uncover as you research your essay for this contest.

Each fall this contest draws participation by thousands of students in U.S. schools. Through the DAR overseas units, both American and non-American students also may enter.

Fifth and sixth graders write 300 to 600 words. You must include a bibliography and a title page. The title page must give the year's topic ("Trails West" was 1996's); an optional title; your name, address, grade, and school; the name of the sponsoring DAR chapter; and the number of words in the essay.

It's up to schools to contact the DAR chapter in their city in order to participate. There's no cost. Each chapter sets its own deadline. The deadlines tend to fall in December, since the chapters must forward winning essays on to the state organizations by mid-January. State winners advance to district competitions. From the eight district winners is chosen the nation's best essay.

The national winners receive cash awards. The essays are published in *DAR Magazine*. Certificates and pins are awarded to chapter, state, and district winners. Rules for the next year's contest appear in the July issue of *DAR Magazine*.

National History Day Competition

Grade 6
Write: National History Day
University of Maryland
0119 Cecil Hall

College Park, MD 20742
E-mail: hstryday@aol.com
Internet: http://www.inform.umd.edu/NHD/
Call: Cathy Gorn, Executive Director
Main: 301-314-9739

National History Day is an exciting way to study history and to learn about issues, ideas, people, and events that interest you. Express what you have learned through a paper, a performance, a museumlike display, or a media presentation.

Begin your research with the sixteen-page contest guide. It lays out the rules in great detail, such as an automatic five-point deduction for performances that exceed time limits. The judges mainly look for quality of research, historical accuracy, analysis and interpretation, a balanced presentation of materials, understanding of historical context, documentation of sources, clarity of presentation, and relevance to the (always broad) annual theme. The 1996–97 theme was "Triumph and Tragedy in History."

You'll first compete in district and state competitions (in some places you begin with state) before proceeding to the national competition, held each June at the University of Maryland at College Park. Check with your state coordinator for deadlines. You can find your state coordinator listed at the National History Day Web site, or call or write to National History Day.

Regular prizes are $1,000, $500, and $250. Each year donors add many special prizes.

Multidiscipline Competitions

Delta's World Adventure® Challenge with Carmen Sandiego™

Ages 9–12
Lifetime Learning Systems, Inc.
Box DE

79 Sanford Street
Fairfield, CT 06430
E-mail: anne@fitzco.com
Internet: http://www.delta-air.com/ffl/adv/adv_win.htm
Call: Anne Milner
Direct: 404-266-7578
Fax: 404-231-1085

The evil Carmen Sandiego has grown bored with globe-trotting. Now she hops around in time as well! You and other "time pilots" are needed to track her down.

Your mission: Create a time capsule with information about a time and place where Carmen stole an object that was making history. Then tell about your shuttle mission back in time to thwart her plans. You'll need to know all about the stolen object. Why was it important? What would happen if it were never returned to history? What were the object's physical surroundings like at that moment? How were language, religion, dress, food, education, and so on different (or not) than they are today?

Based on your research, you'll create a hand-drawn map and one other piece of original artwork. You'll write up to 300 words describing what's in your time capsule. You'll also make a list of the resources used to put the capsule together.

Finally, you get to write a creative story about your journey back in time and capture of Carmen (ages nine and ten: 1,000 to 1,200 words; ages eleven and twelve: 1,300 to 2,000 words). Write neatly, or type if you can. Your essay should be double-spaced and (since all nationalities may enter) written in English.

Submit your time capsule, art, essay, and application form by March 1. Prizes include U.S. Savings Bonds, trips to Space Camp, and more!

Hometown Trees Kids Art Contest

Ages 6–12
Independent Grocers Alliance (IGA)

8725 West Higgins Road
Chicago, IL 60631
Internet: http://www.igainc.com/htm/htppage/treewnnr.stm
Call: Hometown Trees Coordinator
Main: 773-693-4520
Fax: 773-693-1271

They call it an art contest. But the judges look at more than the picture you draw on an IGA grocery sack. They also consider how well your essay answers a question like "If I Was a Tree, What Would I Be?"

Enter between the first of January and mid-March. You can obtain details from the IGA Web site or from your local IGA grocer (2,800 stores in medium-sized cities and rural areas throughout the United States).

Grand prize is a $10,000 college scholarship. Regional winners also receive cash prizes.

Kids Are Authors™

Grades 1–6
Write: Pages BOOK FAIRS
801 Ninety-fourth Avenue North
St. Petersburg, FL 33702
Internet: AOL keyword virgin
Toll free: 800-726-1030

Three or more elementary school students create their own, previously unpublished picture book (story and illustrations). The students must do all the work; no alterations or editing by adults!

Produce eleven pages of typed or handwritten text (fifty words per page maximum) and eleven illustrations, for a total of twenty-two pages. If you want, include a title page, dedication page, and so on. Use one side of the paper only. The size should be at least nine by twelve inches, but not more than eleven by fourteen inches. Send your original art, not photocopies.

Submit your creation along with a copy of the official entry form and a labeled group photo of you, your coauthors, and adult coordinators. Entries are due by mid-March. Entries are not returned. Nor are they acknowledged—unless you win, of course. Entries become the property of Pages, Inc., which gets to publish the winners royalty-free.

Grand prize is $1,000 for the school and $250 for the project coordinator/teacher. Student grand-prize winners receive copies of their published book, engraved medallions, T-shirts, and certificates. They are honored at an awards ceremony.

There are up to five second-place winners. Schools receive $100 and a certificate. Project coordinators receive educational software. Student authors receive certificates.

A third-place winner is named from each state and the District of Columbia. Prizes are software for project coordinators and certificates for student authors.

Knowledge Master Open

Grades 5–6
Write: Academic Hallmarks
P.O. Box 998
Durango, CO 81302
E-mail: greatauk@frontier.net
Internet: http://www.greatauk.com/
Call: Bob Sauer, Contest Coordinator
Toll free: 800-321-9218
Main: 970-247-8738
Fax: 970-247-0997

Imagine teams of students huddled around a computer screen for two hours. No, they aren't playing the latest video game. They are participating in the KMO, a contest that each fall and spring throws 200 multiple-choice questions at student teams in all fifty states and nineteen foreign countries.

The questions, provided on diskette, come from these topics: American history, world history, government, recent events, economics and law, geography, literature, English, math, physical science, biology, earth science, health and psychology, fine arts, and plain old trivia.

Schools pay to register teams. The fee is $35 for either the December or April KMO, or $53 for both. Practice disks are $17.

Past teams have ranged in size from one member to sixty, but ten to fifteen is the norm. Students use teamwork and communication skills to earn points based on both accuracy and speed. Scores are used to rank the teams nationally, by state, and by school size. Plaques and T-shirts are awarded to the top teams.

Sample Questions

1. The islands of Lesbos and Samos are closest to which island?
   A. Cyprus   B. Rhodes   C. Corsica   D. Minorca   E. Sardinia

2. The angstrom is a unit of measurement used to specify . . .
   A. latent heat   B. fluid viscosity   C. stellar distances
   D. magnetic attraction   E. electromagnetic wavelengths

3. Which painting was created first?
   A. *Sunflowers*   B. *The Blue Boy*   C. *View of Toledo*
   D. *The Last Supper*   E. *Christina's World*

4. Goneril, Regan, and Cordelia were daughters of . . .
   A. King Lear   B. King John   C. King Herod   D. King Arthur   E. King Solomon

The National Written & Illustrated by . . . Awards Contest for Students

Ages 6–12
Write: Landmark Editions

P.O. Box 270169
Kansas City, MO 64127
Toll free: 800-653-2665
Main: 816-241-4919
Fax: 816-483-3755

Can you write? Can you draw? You've got to do both in this contest. Landmark Editions will publish the best book that is both written and illustrated by the same student.

Your book must meet lots of requirements relating to number of pages, number of illustrations, size and placement of text, binding, book cover, book jacket, and more. Obtain all rules with the official entry form by sending a no. 10 (business-sized) envelope with sixty-four cents postage.

Write fact or fiction, prose or poetry—it's up to you. Get a teacher or librarian to check for proper spelling and grammar, and even to suggest ways to improve the story line. But don't let anyone alter or rewrite it. The finished book should represent your own skill and imagination.

Entry fee is $1 (although you won't be disqualified if you leave it out). Your teacher or librarian must submit your book.

The postmark deadline is May 1. Winners are notified by mid-October. They are brought to Kansas City and offered a publishing contract. Bear in mind that "99 percent" of the books that Landmark publishes are the winning student books. So Landmark expects them to make money, and you can, too, if your book is selected. It's not unusual for a student author's annual royalty check to greatly exceed $1,000.

Odyssey of the Mind

Grades K–6
Write: OM Association
P.O. Box 547
Glassboro, NJ 08028-0547
Call: Janet d'Alessandro

Main: 609-881-1603, ext. 14
Fax: 609-881-3596

When schools, certified home schools, and formally recognized community groups join the OM Association, they get access to classroom materials that help students develop creative problem-solving skills. Members also get to enter teams of five to seven students in OM competitions, culminating in the World Finals. The OM Association has members in all states and in Canada, Australia, China, Europe, and South America. Cost of annual membership is $135 for North American members, $150 for others.

Each year OM Association provides members with long-term problems for students to solve. The problems cover a wide range of interests. Some are technical, such as designing, building, and driving a vehicle powered by the wind. Others are performance oriented, such as reenactment of a historical event or a scene from classic literature.

🍎 United States Academic Triathlon

Grades 3–6
Write: University of St. Thomas
DUN 234
Minneapolis, MN 55403
E-mail: plsheldon@stthomas.edu
Call: Peggy Sheldon, National Coordinator
Main: 612-962-4534
Fax: 612-962-4810

The United States Academic Triathlon's motto is "Cross-Training for Young Minds." Its events, held in a small-group setting, teach and reinforce creative problem-solving and higher-level thinking skills. Very little coaching by adults is needed.

"P.A.R.T.Y. in a Box" asks five-member student teams to solve a problem and then perform their solution for other teams with provided materials. "Mind Sprints" pose ten-minute problems with verbal, spatial, and mathematical components. "Face-Off!" poses questions from academic subjects, current events, and "kid-summer" issues like what you learn from the nutrition labels on cereal boxes.

Entry fees for the triathlon are $205 for the first team from a school or district, $175 for additional teams. Schools get to participate in at least four meets. They receive copies of problems and a newsletter. And they have the chance to go on to state tournaments. A fairly new competition, the United States Academic Triathlon was active in four states in 1996. If it sounds like fun to you, urge your teacher to start this event at your school.

Mythology

🍎 National Mythology Exam

Grades 3–6
Write: American Classical League
Miami University
Oxford, OH 45056
E-mail: americanclassicalleague@muohio.edu
Internet: http://www.umich.edu/~acleague/
Call: Geri Dutra, Administrative Secretary
Main: 513-529-7741
Fax: 513-529-7742

This test is offered in late February to early March. It covers Greek and Roman as well as Native American and African mythology.

Registration deadline is mid-January. The tests are mailed to your school. Cost is $10 for five, and $2 each after that; your teacher may want to offer the exam to the whole class. Outside the United States, exams cost $3 each. Every student receives a participation ribbon. The top 10 percent get certificates of excellence. The top 5 percent receive bronze medallions.

Social Studies

🍎National Social Studies Olympiad

Look in this chapter, under Current Events section, "Continental Mathematics League."

7

Honor Roll

Academic Talent Searches, Honor Societies, Membership Organizations, and Recognition Awards

Want to make friends who share your interest in carnivorous plants, prime numbers, or moon rocks? You can by joining the membership organizations listed here. Some are open to all; others are honor societies for students with good enough grades.

Also look at the academic talent search organization that serves your state. If you qualify, sign up to get tips on academic opportunities especially for you. There's also a list of very worthwhile recognition awards for all kinds of students. Take a look!

Don't be bashful about seeking help from adults. They devote a lot of thought, effort, and time to helping kids succeed, in school and out. So if you want to start an honor society at your school and need an adult to be the chapter sponsor, just ask. If you think you qualify for a recognition award but need to be nominated by an adult, just ask. They will help you if possible, or assist you in finding another adult who can be of service.

Academic Talent Searches

CTY Talent Search: Fifth and Sixth Grades

Grades 5 and 6
Write: Center for Talented Youth Headquarters
CTY Young Students Talent Search
The Johns Hopkins University
3400 North Charles Street
Baltimore, MD 21218-4319
E-mail: ctyinfo@jhunix.hcf.jhu.edu
Internet: http://www.jhu.edu/~gifted
Call: Phone Bank
Main: 410-516-0337
Direct: 410-516-0278
Fax: 410-516-0804

To apply, you must live in one of these places: Alaska, Arizona, California, Connecticut, Delaware, Hawaii, Maine, Maryland, Massachusetts, New Hampshire, New Jersey, New York, Oregon, Pennsylvania, Rhode Island, Vermont, Virginia, Washington, West Virginia, and the District of Columbia.

In addition, you must show a ninety-seventh or higher national percentile rank related to mathematical or verbal reasoning on your most recent or next-most-recent standardized aptitude or achievement test score report. Virtually all school kids take such tests.

If you meet the residency and test-score qualifications, get an application from the Center for Talented Youth or your guidance counselor. Return it no later than mid-November with the $25 application fee. CTY will then send you a registration booklet for a standardized test called PLUS Academic Abilities Assessment (PLUS). Fill out the PLUS registration form. Return it by early December to Educational Testing Service with a $35 test fee. You take the test in either December or January.

Participation offers several benefits. At the very least, you learn more about your abilities by taking the PLUS test. You get a certificate recognizing your outstanding ability and, if among the top scorers, you are honored at an awards ceremony. Four participants—the fifth and sixth graders with the top math and verbal scores—receive a $1,000 credit toward participation in CTY Young Students Academic Programs. One qualifying participant selected at random gets a full scholarship for those programs.

Midwest Talent Search

Grade 6
Write: Northwestern University
Center for Talent Development
617 Dartmouth Place
Evanston, IL 60208-4175
Internet: http://ctdnet.acns.nwu.edu/
Call: Pat Gaul, Assistant Search Coordinator
Main: 847-491-3782
Fax: 847-467-4283

To apply, you must live in one of these Upper Midwest states: Illinois, Indiana, Michigan, Minnesota, North Dakota, Ohio, South Dakota, and Wisconsin.

Also, you must have scored in the ninety-seventh percentile or better on your most recent nationally normed standardized achievement test (like the Iowa Test of Basic Skills) in the math, verbal, or composite category. Your school doesn't administer such tests? No problem—your parents can nominate you.

Get the application and return it by mid-October, along with a $26 fee. Then take either the SAT I: Reasoning Test for a $21.50 fee or the ACT Assessment for $19.

A score in the ninety-fifth percentile or above earns you recognition at an awards ceremony, career guidance, and invitations to summer programs. CTD even gives you unlimited access to the Internet.

Motivation for Academic Performance

Grades 4 and 5
Write: Duke University
P.O. Box 90780
Durham, NC 27708-0780
Call: Patricia Hege, Search Coordinator
Direct: 919-683-1400
Fax: 919-683-1742

MAP focuses on students living in these southern and midwestern states: Alaska, Arkansas, Florida, Georgia, Iowa, Kansas, Kentucky, Louisiana, Mississippi, Missouri, Nebraska, North Carolina, Oklahoma, South Carolina, Tennessee, and Texas.

You may sign up for MAP if you have scored at the ninety-fifth percentile or better in math, verbal, or composite on a standardized test. The program costs $16. You will receive a MAP certificate of achievement. And you will have the option of taking an out-of-level test (designed for eighth graders, in fact) to highlight your academic strengths. The test costs $21. The remainder of the program consists of mailings from MAP that will alert you to academic competitions, academic summer programs, and other resources.

Rocky Mountain Talent Search

Grade 6
Write: University of Denver
Center for Educational Services
2135 East Wesley Avenue
Denver, CO 80208
Call: Rich Radcliffe, Director
Main: 303-871-2983
Fax: 303-871-3422

Participation is open to "academically able and highly motivated" students from Rocky Mountain states: Colorado, Idaho, Montana, Nevada, New Mexico, Utah, and Wyoming.

Such students must meet *any one* of the following criteria:

★   Maintain an A average at school all year.
★   Score in the ninetieth percentile in a major subject area on a standardized test. The score can't be more than five years old.
★   Obtain a recommendation by a teacher or counselor.

Applicants should also have experience taking long standardized tests, or have the attention span or other skills to do well.

To apply, request an application from RMTS and return it from mid-November to mid-January. There's a $25 fee, plus the test fee of $19 for the ACT Assessment or $21.50 for the SAT I: Reasoning Test.

Score high enough, and you will be invited to take fast-paced classes at the Summer Institute at the University of Denver. You'll also qualify to attend the summer programs of other talent searches.

Honor Societies

🍎 American Technology Honor Society

Grade 6; home schools ineligible
Write: Technology Student Association
1914 Association Drive
Reston, VA 20191-1540
E-mail: aths@nassp.org
Internet: http://www.nassp.org/aths
Call: Hillary Lee
Main: 703-860-9000
Fax: 703-758-4852

The American Technology Honor Society recognizes students for achievement in four ATHS membership criteria areas: technological literacy, including the creative and responsible use of technology; scholarship; commitment to service; and leadership. Individual secondary schools establish chapters of ATHS by chartering with the national office. Eligible schools must have Internet access or plans to establish such access. If your school has no chapter, talk to a teacher about starting one.

A student may be nominated as an ATHS candidate upon completion of the first semester of middle school that begins with sixth grade. A candidate is nominated based upon potential to meet the membership criteria. A candidate advances to the associate level of membership once the criteria are met. The highest level of membership—the scholar status—is awarded in the junior or senior year to those students who demonstrate exceptional achievement in the criteria areas.

Firestone Firehawks

Ages 5–12
Write: Bridgestone/Firestone
50 Century Boulevard
Nashville, TN 37219
Call: Ann Ewing, Program Coordinator
Main: 615-872-1410
Direct: 615-780-3330
Fax: 615-872-1414

Each year about 100 kids nationwide are chosen for membership in recognition of their outstanding environmental efforts. Since the Firestone Firehawk honors club was established in 1991, some 500 members have been inducted.

One Firehawk, Nisa Mason of Boerne, Texas, took part in her first environmental cause when she was eight. She helped persuade her city council not to turn a field of native tall-grass prairie into a baseball field.

Three Illinois students were inducted into the Firehawks for their work on a project called the Prairie Lakes Biofilter. They spent a year studying water quality, monitoring plant life, and initiating cleanup of the area.

An adult nominates a student for his or her eco-activism. The nomination form has sections that are filled out by the nominator, the student, and the student's parent or guardian. Submit the form by early April.

Firehawks receive a club T-shirt, a newsletter, and other memorabilia. They vow to continue to seek opportunities to be advocates for ecology.

🍎 National Junior Forensic League

Grade 6; home schools ineligible
Write: National Forensic League
P.O. Box 38
Ripon, WI 54971-0038
Call: James Copeland, Executive Secretary
Main: 414-748-6206

The National Junior Forensic League (and its high school counterpart, the National Forensic League) encourages students to become proficient in the forensic arts: debate, public speaking, and interpretation. Members earn points and degrees for speaking and debate activities.

Former president Lyndon Johnson was an alumnus of the National Forensic League. Other notable alumni include former vice president Hubert Humphrey; former senators David Boren and Karl Mundt; Senator Richard Lugar; Supreme Court Justice Stephen Breyer; and from the fields of journalism and entertainment: Don Ameche, Tom Brokaw, James Dean, Kelsey Grammer, Rush Limbaugh, Shelley Long, Jane Pauley, Ted Turner, and Oprah Winfrey.

Membership Organizations

🍎 Chi Alpha Mu

Grade 6
Write: Chi Alpha Mu

Tulsa Community College
3727 East Apache
Tulsa, OK 74115
E-mail: jhammon@vm.tulsa.cc.ok.us
Call: Jane Hammontree, XAM Secretary
Main: 918-595-7000
Direct: 918-595-7481
Fax: 918-595-7598

Are you nimble with numbers? Meet more kids like yourself and find out about fun math competitions by joining Chi Alpha Mu, also known as the National Junior Mathematics Club. Chapters are found in 80 to 100 schools. Activities vary by school but are related to the enjoyment and promotion of interest in mathematics. Contact the headquarters in Tulsa to learn how to start a chapter in your school.

There is no GPA requirement to join. Five-member teams from each club compete in the Math Bowl test each spring. Awards are medals and plaques. The top eight students form two teams at the annual spring convention for a math showdown.

Clover Kids and 4-H

Grades K–6
Write: National 4-H Council
7100 Connecticut Avenue
Chevy Chase, MD 20815

Maybe 4-H brings to mind raising a lamb for the local livestock show. But the fact is that even city kids in the third grade or higher join 4-H (students in kindergarten through second grade join Clover Kids). In some states only one member in four lives in a rural area or town smaller than 10,000.

4-H offers projects in more than forty subject areas, from horses, photography, wildlife, public speaking, and bicycles to small engines, dairy cattle, computer science, forestry, and automobiles. 4-H also sponsors a score of school curriculum enrichment programs.

Joining 4-H costs little or nothing. Some projects may require an investment to get started.

🍎 Junior Beta Club

Grades 5 and 6
Write: National Beta Club
151 West Lee Street
Spartanburg, SC 29306-3012
E-mail: betaclub@betaclub.org
Internet: http://www.betaclub.org/
Call: Growth and Development Department
Toll free: 800-845-8281
Main: 864-583-4554

This club and its high school counterpart, the Senior Beta Club, recognize students for their academic achievements and their good character, leadership, and service to others.

President Bill Clinton is a National Beta Club alumnus. The club has 300,000-plus active members and more than 4 million alumni.

Each affiliated school decides what the scholastic or service requirements will be for its chapter. At least five students are needed to start a chapter. Students pay a one-time membership fee of $10. There is no charge to the school for chartering a Beta Club. Activities include annual conventions that feature academic competitions such as quiz bowls.

🍎 Technology Student Association

Grade 6
Write: Technology Student Association
1914 Association Drive
Reston, VA 20191

Internet: http://tmn.com/Organizations/Iris/tsawww/tsa.html
Call: Sandy Honour
Main: 703-860-9000
Fax: 703-758-4852

Membership in TSA is open to students who take or have taken technology classes in their middle school or high school. (Some middle schools begin with grade 6.) Such classes might involve hands-on experience in photography, television broadcasting, robotics, synthetic materials, rocketry, lasers, ergonomics, and much more. Currently there are 150,000 members in forty-three states.

After completing their technology projects during the school year, students travel to an annual conference within the United States. There they compete with other students from around the country at TSA's Competitive Events Program. The fifty events involve topics such as aerospace, architecture, speech, graphic design, and a "Technology Bowl." One event asks contestants to design, draw, and build a CO_2-powered vehicle.

TSA also helps students learn to work closely as part of a team, develop leadership skills, and recognize the importance of service to the community.

Young America

Up to age 12
Write: National Junior Horticultural Association
1424 North Eighth Street
Durant, OK 74701
E-mail: smax@isc-durant.com
Call: Joe Maxson, Executive Secretary
Main: 405-924-0771
Fax: 405-924-6337

Got a green thumb, or just wish you did? Horticulture concerns itself with growing vegetables, fruits, flowers, ornamental plants, nuts, herbs, and turf. It is to your yard what agriculture is to a farmer's field. Young America and NJHA (which serves students age fifteen and older) exist to give all kids an appreciation of horticulture and to acquaint them with career opportunities in that industry.

Joining is free. Fill out a form, send it in, and you're a member. Some 5,000 young people currently belong. Membership entitles you to participate in contests in gardening, plant propagation (making many plants from one), environmental beautification, and experimental horticulture. There's an essay competition as well.

❦Young Astronaut Club

Grades K–6
Write: Young Astronaut Council
1308 Nineteenth Street NW
Washington, DC 20036
E-mail: yacl@aol.com
Toll free: 800-626-2345
Main: 202-682-1984
Fax: 202-775-1773

Probably nothing puts mankind's math and science skills to the test like space travel. The Young Astronaut Club is for future space explorers who want fun and challenging ways to learn about the scientific principles that will put them in orbit.

For a $40 annual fee, a teacher can start a Young Astronaut chapter with up to thirty students. The fee covers curriculum materials and enables students to participate in contests. For instance, a contest in 1995–96 asked chapters to send a list of five images and five sounds that ought to be recorded and sent into space to tell aliens about earthlings.

Students without access to a chapter may also join the club individually and still participate in contests. The cost is $16 for individual members, plus $10 each for any additional family members wishing to join.

Recognition Awards

🍎 Daughters of the American Revolution Awards

Grades K–6; home schools ineligible
Write: National Society Daughters of the American Revolution
1776 D Street NW
Washington, DC 20006-5392
Call: Caroline Hopkins
Main: 202-879-3253
Fax: 202-879-3252

1. GOOD CITIZENSHIP MEDAL
Good Citizenship Medals are presented to students who demonstrate the qualities of honor, service, courage, leadership, and patriotism. Schools elect whether or not to participate in this no-cost program.

2. JUNIOR AMERICAN CITIZENS
The purpose of the Junior American Citizens club is to encourage the teaching of children of all races and creeds the principles of good citizenship. Many schools incorporate the cost-free JAC program into their special studies classes and homerooms.

Membership is free for students. Membership cards, pins, and other supplies are furnished by the National Society DAR.

Global 500 Youth Environment Award

Ages 6–12
Write: United Nations Environment Programme
Attn: Secretary of the Global 500 Roll of Honor
P.O. Box 30552

Nairobi, Kenya
E-mail: sniffen@un.org
Internet: http://www.unep.org/
Call: Jim Sniffen, UNEP-New York
Main: 212-963-8210
Direct: 212-963-8094
Fax: 212-963-7341

Kids around the world are your competitors in this award! UNEP believes that young people are important partners and allies in raising environmental awareness and triggering environmental action. This award recognizes those who have done something outstanding in the field of environmental protection. Only a handful are selected each year.

Individuals or groups may be nominated, but not self-nominated. Nominators fill out a form in which they summarize in 250 words the nominee's environmental achievements. Nominators should include any updated literature, press stories, and two references other than that of the nominator. Nomination forms must be received by December 31.

Nominees should have:

★ contributed to the protection, restoration, and enhancement of the environment;

★ successfully solved a specific environmental problem or otherwise significantly advanced the cause of the environment;

★ succeeded in bringing to public notice significant environmental issues or in mobilizing local or national action toward their solution;

★ demonstrated the potential to serve as a model to others.

Awards are made in these areas: energy efficiency, forest protection, community cleanup, renewable energy, environmental beautification, community environmental education, transportation efficiency, soil conservation, institutional environmental education, air pollution reduction, wildlife and flora conservation, public awareness, freshwater protection, waste reduction, environmental health and sanitation, marine conservation, recycling, and other.

JCPenney Golden Rule Award

Up to age 12
Write: JCPenney
Community Relations
P.O. Box 10001
Dallas, TX 75301-8101
E-mail: BCAGE@jcpenney.com
Call: Brenda Cage, Community Relations
Main: 214-431-1319
Fax: 214-431-1355

In 1902 in the Wyoming town of Kemmerer, James Cash Penney opened his first store and named it the Golden Rule. The name reflected the future retail magnate's belief in involvement in community service ("Do unto Others as You Would Have Them Do unto You").

The JCPenney Golden Rule Award recognizes the efforts of individual and group volunteers in more than 220 communities nationwide. The volunteers are nominated by their peers and chosen by local civic leaders.

In its youth category, a local youth is chosen and $1,000 is contributed to his or her nonprofit organization of choice. Winners are eligible for the annual JCPenney National Golden Rule Award and a chance to win an additional $5,000 contribution and a $5,000 scholarship. Call to learn whether the program is active in your community.

Kids' Hall of Fame

Up to age 12; U.S. citizens only
Write: National Geographic World and Pizza Hut
Dept. Hall of Fame—JG

P.O. Box 96000
Washington, DC 20090-6000
Call: Emily Foshee
Main: 202-775-6112
Direct: 214-338-7643
Fax: 214-338-7689

If you think you belong in the Kids' Hall of Fame, you can pick up a nomination form next time you visit Pizza Hut. Send it in between November and mid-March. Tell what outstanding deed you did or what significant contribution you made to your family, school, state, country, or planet. Past winners raised funds for charity, supported peers with life-threatening diseases, and fought for historic preservation.

Six young people a year are inducted, which earns them each a $10,000 scholarship. Another six finalists and 200 first- and second-place winners are recognized.

National Awards Program

Grades K–6
Write: Freedoms Foundation at Valley Forge
Route 23
Valley Forge, PA 19482-0706
Call: Christy Pierce
Main: 610-933-8825
Fax: 610-935-0522

The National Awards Program was established to honor exceptional efforts of those who promote an understanding of responsible citizenship and the benefits of a free society. In the youth category, entries can be almost anything—poems, essays, a description of volunteer activity, and so forth. Entrants can be self-nominated, but usually they are nominated by a parent, teacher, or guidance counselor.

A recent top winner was a sixth grader in Chattanooga, Tennessee. For a class project, she gathered information on the role of women in

World War II. With her mother's help, she advertised to get stories from women. The response was overwhelming. And having discovered each other through the student's project, the women who responded formed an association called Women of WWII, built a memorial, and held a parade.

The top winner gets a $100 U.S. Savings Bond and a four-inch medallion of George Washington.

National Conservation Achievement Awards

Grades K–6
Write: National Wildlife Federation
Attn: Public Affairs Department
8925 Leesburg Pike
Vienna, VA 22184-0001
Internet: http://www.nwf.org/
Call: Public Affairs Department
Main: 703-790-4085

The National Wildlife Federation is the nation's largest environmental education organization. It created the National Conservation Achievement Awards in 1965 to recognize individuals and organizations for their accomplishments in natural resource conservation.

The youth category is open to individuals or groups of young people who demonstrate commitment to conserving natural resources and protecting the environment.

Nomination deadline is mid-June. Winners are honored at an awards banquet at the NWF annual meeting in the spring.

President's Education Awards Program

Grade 6; home schools ineligible
Write: United States Department of Education

President's Education Awards Program
6000 Independence Avenue SW
Washington, DC 20202
Call: Linda Bugg, Director of Program
Toll free: 800-438-7232
Main: 202-401-3644
Fax: 202-401-1368

Recognition by the president of the United States? You can't do much better than that!

Your first step is to make sure your school participates in this program. If it does, the Department of Education gives your school certificates at no charge to be awarded to qualifying students. So cost is no excuse for a school not to take part. (Schools may buy optional lapel pin awards for a modest price.) Your school counselor should know where things stand.

Your second step is to quality for an award. Get going!

1. PRESIDENT'S AWARD FOR EDUCATIONAL EXCELLENCE

To be eligible, you must have a GPA of 3.5 (on a 4.0-point scale). Also, you must have scored in the eighty-fifth percentile in math and reading on a standardized test or be recommended by a teacher and another school staff member as an outstanding achiever.

2. PRESIDENT'S AWARD FOR EDUCATIONAL IMPROVEMENT

This award isn't for students who already do well, but for those who having been doing much better lately. For instance, a student who shows tremendous growth and improvement but does not meet the criteria for the President's Award for Educational Excellence might be given this award. Or it might go to a student who demonstrates unusual commitment to learning and improving in academics despite various obstacles.

The award is given whenever the principal thinks someone has earned it. If you think you qualify, speak up!

Young Citizenship Award

Grades K–6; U.S. citizens only
Write: National Exchange Club
3050 Central Avenue
Toledo, OH 43606-1700
E-mail: nechq@aol.com
Internet: http://rtpnet.org/~nec/
Call: Laurie Milosch, Programs Coordinator
Toll free: 800-924-2643
Main: 419-535-3232, ext. 123
Fax: 419-535-1989

The National Exchange Club exists to serve. More than 1,100 local branches undertake volunteer projects that benefit their communities.

You don't have to be the star student or athlete to win this award. Just be honest, hardworking, helpful, and fair—all qualities of excellent citizenship. Winners are chosen by their teachers. Their local Exchange Club presents them with a certificate. Contact your local club for details, or contact the national headquarters to find the club nearest you.

Index